Knitability

Fun knits for all the family

Linda O'Brien and Gyles Brandreth

COLLINS

Acknowledgements

The authors and publishers would like to express their grateful thanks to the following people:

Photography
Francis Loney, assisted by Steve Nichols

Make-up
Karen Purvis

Hair
Peter Kenny

Knitters
Sybil Bell
Linda Blackman
Barbara Chevalier
Avril Crawford
Gladys Ketteringham
Philippa Lewis
Marian Pammenter

Sheep kindly supplied by Hamish Macnab at Four Seasons

SPECIAL THANKS

Special thanks are due to our models:
Lionel Blair
Aphra Brandreth
Benet Brandreth
Saethryd Brandreth
Michèle Brown
Lynsey de Paul
Fiona Hendley
Aled Jones
Paul Jones
Sarah Kennedy
Emma Lewis
George Lewis
Sophie Lewis
Nanette Newman
Francesca O'Brien
Peter O'Brien
Su Pollard
Anneka Rice
Ben Webb
Lizzie Webb
who generously donated their modelling fees to the National Playing Fields Association, the charity that helps preserve, create and improve playgrounds and play space for children and young people throughout the country, especially the disadvantaged and the disabled. If you too would like to help the NPFA's important work please write to 25 Ovington Square, London, SW3 1LQ.

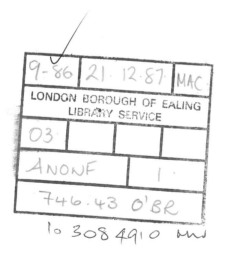
First published 1987 by
William Collins Sons & Co Ltd
London · Glasgow · Sydney
Auckland · Toronto · Johannesburg
© Gyles Brandreth/Linda O'Brien 1987

British Library Cataloguing in Publication Data
O'Brien, Linda
Knitability.
1. Knitting—Patterns
I. Title   II. Brandreth, Gyles
746.43'2041   TT820

ISBN 0 00 412242 9

Photoset by V & M Graphics Ltd, Aylesbury, Bucks.
Printed and bound in Singapore by
Tien Wah Press Ltd

Illustrations by Sara Sliwinska
Pattern grids by Clive Sutherland

Contents

Useful Addresses

Yarn Suppliers

Argyll Wools Ltd
PO Box 15
Priestley Mills
Pudsey
W. Yorks LS28 9LT
Tel. 0532 558411

Hayfield Textiles Ltd
Glusburn
Keighley
W. Yorks BD20 8QP
Tel. 0535 33333

Lister
George Lee and Sons Ltd
PO Box 37
Whiteoak Mills
Wakefield
W. Yorks WF2 9SF
Tel. 0924 375311

Patons and Baldwin
McMullen Rd
Darlington
Co. Durham DL1 1YQ
Tel. 0325 381010

Sirdar PLC
Flanshaw Lane
Alverthorpe
Wakefield
W. Yorks WF2 9ND
Tel. 0924 371501

**Patons and Baldwin
Overseas Suppliers**

USA
Susan Bates Inc.
212 Middlesex Ave.
Chester
Connecticut 06412

Canada
Patons and Baldwin (Canada) Inc.
1001 Roselawn Ave.
Toronto
Ontario M6B 1B8

Australia
Coats Patons (Australia) Ltd
PO Box 110
Fern Tree Gully Rd
Mount Waverley
Victoria

New Zealand
Coats Patons (New Zealand) Ltd
263 Ti Racall Drive
Pakuranga
Auckland

South Africa
Patons and Baldwin PSA (Pty) Ltd
PO Box 33
Randfonteine 1760
Transvaal

Knit Kits

Knitability
Flintwood
Leas Green
Chislehurst
Kent BR7 6HD
Tel. 01 300 5104

BEAD SUPPLIERS

Mail order

The Button Box
44 Bedford St
Covent Garden
London WC2E 9HA
Tel. 01 240 2716/2841

Creative Beadcraft Ltd
Unit 26
Chiltern Trading Estate
Earl Howe Rd
Holmer Green
High Wycombe
Bucks HP15 6QT
Tel. 0494 715606

Hobby Horse Ltd
15–17 Langton St
London SW10 0JL
Tel. 01 351 1913/3472

Personal shoppers

Ells and Farrier Ltd
5 Princes St
Hanover Sq
London W1R 8PH
Tel. 01 629 9964

YARN CONVERSION CHART

	UK	USA/Canada	Australia
Argyll	Laser DK Fluffy Chunky	Laser DK Fluffy Chunky	Laser DK Fluffy Chunky
Hayfield	Grampian DK	Grampian DK	Grampian DK
Lister	Aran Richmond DK	Aran Richmond DK	Aran Richmond DK
Patons	Diploma DK Vision	Beehive DK Moorland DK Promise	Bluebell 8-ply Totem 8-ply Amour
Sirdar	Nocturne Country Style	Nocturne Country Style	Nocturne Country Style

Neckband

Join right shoulder seam.
With 3¼mm. needles and B and RS facing, pick up and K 21 sts. down left front neck, K 16 sts. from stitch holder, pick up and K 21 sts. up right front neck, K 4 sts. down right back neck, K 30 sts. from stitch holder and finally pick up and K 4 sts. up left back neck. (96 sts.)
Work in K1, P1, rib for 12 rows.
Cast off fairly loosely ribwise.

TO MAKE UP

Press according to ball band instructions.
Join left shoulder and neckband seam. Fold neckband in half to inside the slip stitch loosely in position. Measure and mark 23(23: 23: 24: 24: 24)cm. (9(9: 9: 9½: 9½: 9½)in.) each side of shoulder seam and sew sleeves between these marks. Join side and sleeve seams.

= A (peacock blue)
= B (emerald green)
X = C (yellow)
□ = D (red)
● = E (light brown)
✻ = F (dark brown)
O = G (cream)

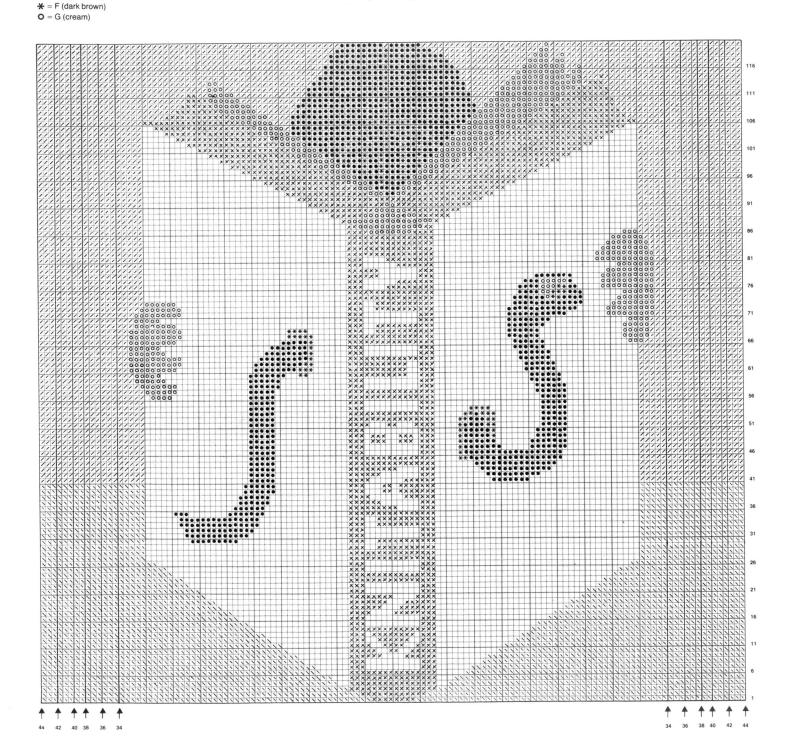

'This Big'

*I*f you know a fisherman who is fond of telling tall stories – fishy tales they're called in angling circles – this is the jumper to knit for him. It's being modelled by a bloke with a whale of a talent: actor, singer, charmer Paul Jones.

MATERIALS

3 100g balls of ARGYLL LASER DK in blue, main colour (C).
1(1: 2: 2: 2: 2) balls in light green, 1st contrast (A).
1 ball in each of 5 other contrasting colours: jade (B); bottle green (D); yellow (E); orange (F) and white (G).
1 pair each of 3¼mm. (No. 10) and

4mm. (No. 8) knitting needles.
2 stitch holders.
The quantities of yarn given are based on average requirements and are therefore approximate.

MEASUREMENTS

To fit bust/chest: 86(91: 96: 101: 107: 112)cm. (34(36: 38: 40: 42: 44)in.)
Actual measurement: 91(96: 102: 106: 111: 116)cm. (36(38½: 40¾: 42: 44: 46½)in.)
Length from shoulder: 64(67: 69: 72: 72: 72)cm. (25¼(26¼: 27¼: 28¼: 28¼: 28¼)in.)
Sleeve length: 48(48: 48: 51: 51: 51)cm. (19(19: 19: 20: 20: 20)in.)
Figures in brackets refer to the larger sizes. Where only one figure is given this refers to all sizes.

TENSION

22 sts. and 29 rows to 10cm. (4in.) on 4mm. needles over st. st.

ABBREVIATIONS

K = knit: **P** = purl; **st.(s.)** = stitch(es); **st. st.** = stocking stitch; **foll.** = following; **inc.** = increase: **dec.** = decrease; **cont.** = continue: **RS** = right side; **WS** = wrong side; **rep.** = repeat; **rem.** = remaining; **DK** = double knitting; **C** = main colour; **A,B,D,E,F,G** = contrast colours; **mm.** = millimetres; **cm.** = centimetres; **in.** = inches.

INSTRUCTIONS

Back
With 3¼mm. needles and A, cast on 82(88: 94: 98: 104: 110)sts. and work in K1, P1, rib for 20 rows.
Change to 4mm. needles.
Increase row: K6(9: 12: 14: 17: 20), inc. in next st., *K3, inc. in next st., rep. from * to last 7(10: 13: 15: 18: 21)sts., K to end of row. (100(106: 112: 116: 122: 128)sts.)
Next row: P.**
Now starting with a K row work straight in st. st. for 48(54: 60: 66: 66: 66) rows, thus ending with a WS row.
Change to B and starting with a K row, work in st. st. for 34 rows.
Change to C and starting with a K row, cont. in st. st. and C only until back

measures 62(65: 67: 70: 70: 70)cm. (24½(25½: 26½: 27½: 27½: 27½)in.) from cast-on edge, ending with a WS row.
Shape back neck
Next row: K35(38: 41: 43: 46: 49)sts., turn and cont. on this first set of sts. only, placing rem. sts. on a stitch holder.
***Dec. 1 st. at neck edge on next 3 rows.
Cast off rem. 32(35: 38: 40: 43: 46)sts. fairly loosely.
Return to rem. sts. and slip first 30 sts. onto stitch holder. With RS facing rejoin yarn to rem. sts. and K to end of row.
Now work as for first side from *** to end.

Front
Work as for back to **
Now starting with a K row work straight in st. st. for 8(14: 20: 26: 26: 26) rows.
Place chart
1st row: (RS facing) K2(5: 8: 10: 13: 16)A. Now work across the 96 sts. of 1st row of **Chart 1**, K2(5: 8: 10: 13: 16)A.
Now cont. to work from chart in st. st. as now placed until the 122 rows have been worked, thus ending with a WS row, and working extra sts. at side edges to correspond with chart.
Now cont. straight in C until front measures 56(59: 61: 64: 64: 64) cm. (22(23: 24: 25: 25: 25)in.) from cast-on edge, ending with a WS row.
Shape front neck
Next row: K42(45: 48: 50: 53: 56)sts., turn and cont. on this first set of sts. only, placing rem. sts. on a stitch holder.
****Dec. 1 st. at neck edge on every row until 32(35: 38: 40: 43: 46)sts. remain. Now cont. straight in st. st. until front measures the same as back to cast-off shoulder edge, ending with a WS row.
Cast off all sts. fairly loosely.
Return to rem. sts. and slip first 16 sts. onto stitch holder. With RS facing rejoin yarn to rem. sts. and K to end of row.
Now work as for first side from **** to end.

Cloud Sleeve
With 3¼mm. needles and C, cast on 44 sts. and work in K1, P1, rib for 20 rows.
Change to 4mm. needles.

Increase row: K2, inc. in next st., *K1, inc. in next st., rep. from * to last 3 sts., K to end. (64 sts.)
Now starting with a P row cont. in st. st., inc. 1 st. at each end of every foll. 6th row until there are 88 sts. on the needle, ending with a WS row.//
Place chart
Next row: K14C, now work across the 60 sts. of 1st row of **Chart 2**, K14C.
Still keeping incs. as before, work the 36 rows from **Chart 2** as shown until there are 94(94: 94: 100: 100: 100)sts. on the needle.
When all incs. are worked and chart is complete. cont. straight in st. st. in C until sleeve measures 48(48: 48: 51: 51: 51)cm. (19(19: 19: 20: 20: 20)in.) from cast-on edge, ending with a WS row. Cast off all sts. fairly loosely.

Sun Sleeve
Work as for cloud sleeve to //.
Place chart
Next row: K33C, now work across the 22 sts. of 1st row of **Chart 3**, K33C. Complete the 30 rows of chart, and finish as for cloud sleeve.

Neckband
Join right shoulder seam.
With 3¼mm. needles and C and RS facing, pick up and K21 sts. down left front neck, K16 sts. from stitch holder, pick up and K21 sts. up right front neck, 4 sts. down right back neck, K30 sts. from stitch holder and finally pick up and K4 sts. up left back neck. (96 sts.)
Work in K1, P1, rib for 12 rows.
Cast off fairly loosely ribwise.

TO MAKE UP

Press according to ball band instructions.
Join left shoulder and neckband seam. Fold neckband in half to inside and slip stitch loosely in position. Measure and mark 23(23: 23: 24: 24: 24)cm. 9(9: 9: 9½: 9½: 9½:)in. each side of shoulder seam and sew sleeves between these marks. Using a chain stitch and E embroider sun's rays and with D embroider eye for fish. Join side and sleeve seams.

Chart 1

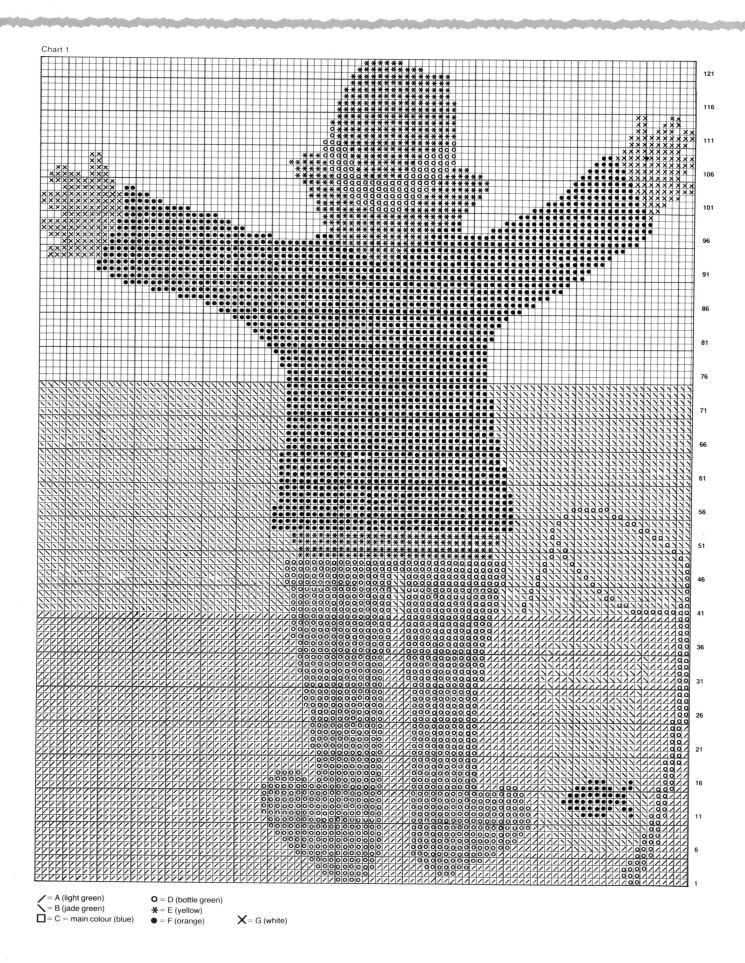

↗ = A (light green)   **O** = D (bottle green)

↘ = B (jade green)   ✱ = E (yellow)

☐ = C = main colour (blue)   ● = F (orange)   ✕ = G (white)

Chart 2

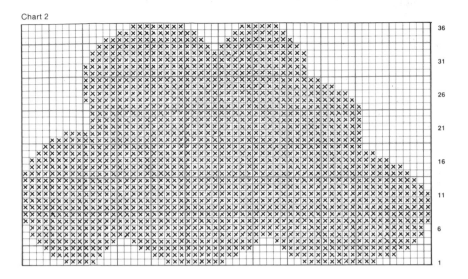

/ = A (light green)
\ = B (jade green)
☐ = C = main colour (blue)
O = D (bottle green)
✻ = E (yellow)
● = F (orange)
X = G (white)

Chart 3

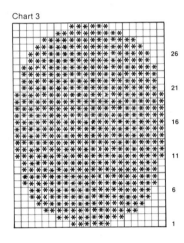

Evening Waistcoat

Fiona Hendley used to be simply a bedazzlingly beautiful and tantalisingly talented actress. She still is. But now she's a bedazzlingly beautiful and tantalisingly talented knitwear model as well. And this stylish fun knit, perfect on Fiona, looks good on the gentlemen, too.

MATERIALS

11(11: 12: 12: 12: 13) 25g balls of DOUBLE KNITTING yarn in 1st colour, white (A).
5(5: 5: 6: 6: 6) balls in 2nd colour, charcoal grey (B).
1 ball in each of 3 other colours, black (C), red (D) and yellow (E).
1 pair each of 3¼mm. (No. 10) and 4mm. (No. 8) knitting needles.
3 stitch holders.
The quantities of yarn given are based on average requirements and are therefore approximate.

MEASUREMENTS

To fit bust / chest: 86(91: 96: 101: 107: 112)cm. (34(36: 38: 40: 42: 44)in.)
Actual measurement: 91(97: 102: 106: 111: 117)cm. (36(38½: 40¾: 42: 44¼: 46½)in.)
Length from shoulder: 63(66: 68: 71: 71: 71)cm. (25(26: 27: 28: 28: 28)in.)
Sleeve length: 48(48: 48: 51: 51: 51)cm. (19(19: 19: 20: 20: 20)in.)
Figures in brackets refer to the larger sizes. Where only one figure is given this refers to all sizes.

TENSION

22 sts. and 28 rows to 10cm. (4in.) on 4 mm. needles over st. st.

ABBREVIATIONS

K = knit; **P** = purl; **st.(s.)** = stitch(es); **st. st.** = stocking stitch; **foll.** = following; **inc.** = increase; **dec.** = decrease; **cont.** = continue; **RS** = right side; **WS** = wrong side; **rep.** = repeat; **rem.** = remaining; **A,B,C,D,E** = contrast colours; **mm.** = millimetres; **cm.** = centimetres; **in.** = inches.

Note
The lines of the shirt front frill, worked in C, may be embroidered or swiss-darned when work is complete rather than knitted, if preferred.

INSTRUCTIONS

Back
With 3¼mm. needles and A, cast on 82(88: 94: 98: 104: 110)sts. and work in K1, P1, rib for 18 rows.
Change to 4mm. needles.

Increase row: K6(9: 12: 14: 17: 20), inc. in next st., *K3, inc. in next st., rep. from * to last 7(10: 13: 15: 18: 21)sts., K to end of row. (100(106: 112: 116: 122: 128)sts.)
Next row: P. **
Now starting with a K row work straight in st. st. in A for 34(42: 48: 56: 56: 56) rows, thus ending with a WS row.

Place chart
Now starting with the 1st row work in st. st. from **Chart 1**, working between appropriate lines for size required. Cont. straight as set until 118 rows of chart have been worked, thus ending with a WS row.

Shape back neck
Next row: (119th row of chart) Patt. 35(38: 41: 43: 46: 49)sts., turn and cont. on this first set of sts. only, placing rem. sts. on a stitch holder.
*** Dec. 1 st. at neck edge on next 3 rows.
Cast off rem. 32(35: 38: 40: 43: 46) sts. fairly loosely. (122 rows of chart complete.) Return to rem. sts. and slip first 30 sts. onto stitch holder. With RS facing rejoin appropriate yarn to rem. sts. and patt. to end of row. Now work as for first side from *** to end.

Front
Work as for back to **
Now starting with a K row straight in st. st. in A for 6(14: 20: 28: 28: 28:) rows, thus ending with a WS row.

Place chart
Now starting with the 1st row, work in st. st. from **Chart 2**, working between appropriate lines for size required. Cont. straight as set until 40 rows of chart have been worked, thus ending with a WS row.

Mock pocket opening
Next row: (41st row of chart) Patt. 8(11: 14: 16: 19: 22)sts., place next 34 sts. onto a stitch holder and leave at front of work, then with B cast on 34 sts., and patt. to end of row. Now cont. working from chart across all sts. until 132nd row of chart has been worked, thus ending with a WS row.

Shape front neck
Next row: (133rd row of chart) Patt. 42(45: 48: 50: 53: 56)sts., turn and cont. on this first set of sts. only, placing rem. sts. on a stitch holder.
**** Keeping chart correct, dec. 1 st. at neck edge on every row until 32(35: 38: 40: 43: 46)sts. remain.
Now cont. straight until chart is com-plete (front measures same as back to cast-off shoulder edge).
Cast off all sts. fairly loosely.
Return to rem. sts. and slip first 16 sts. onto stitch holder. With RS facing rejoin appropriate yarn to rem. sts. and patt. to end of row.
Now work as for first side from **** to end.

Pocket Welt
With 3¼mm. needles and C and RS facing, pick up the 34 sts. from stitch holder and work in K1, P1, rib for 6 rows. Cast off fairly loosely ribwise.

Sleeves
With 3¼mm. needles and A, cast on 44 sts., and work in K1, P1, rib for 18 rows. Change to 4mm. needles.
Increase row: K2, inc. in next st., *K1, inc. in next st., rep. from * to last 3 sts., K to end. (64 sts.)
Now starting with a P row work in st. st. in A, **at the same time**, inc. 1 st. at each end of every foll. 6th row until there are 94(94: 94: 100: 100: 100)sts. on the needle.
Now work straight in st. st. until sleeve measures 48(48: 48: 51: 51: 51)cm. (19(19: 19: 20: 20: 20)in.) from cast-on edge, ending with a WS row.
Cast off all sts. fairly loosely.

Neckband
Join right shoulder seam.
With 3¼mm. needles and A and RS facing, pick up and K21 sts. down left front neck, K16 sts. from stitch holder, pick up and K21 sts. up right front neck, K4 sts. down right back neck, K30 sts. from stitch holder and finally pick up and K4 sts. up left back neck. (96 sts.)
Work in K1, P1, rib for 12 rows.
Cast off fairly loosely ribwise.

TO MAKE UP

Press according to ball band instructions.
Join left shoulder and neckband seam. Fold neckband in half to inside and slip stitch loosely in position. Measure and mark 23(23: 23: 24: 24: 24)cm. 9(9: 9: 9½: 9½: 9½)in. each side of shoulder seam and sew sleeves between these marks. Sew side edges of mock pocket welt neatly to front, and sew cast-on edge neatly to base of mock pocket. Join side and sleeve seams.

/ = A (white)
□ = B (charcoal grey)
\ = C (black)
X = D (red)
● = E (yellow)

Chart 1

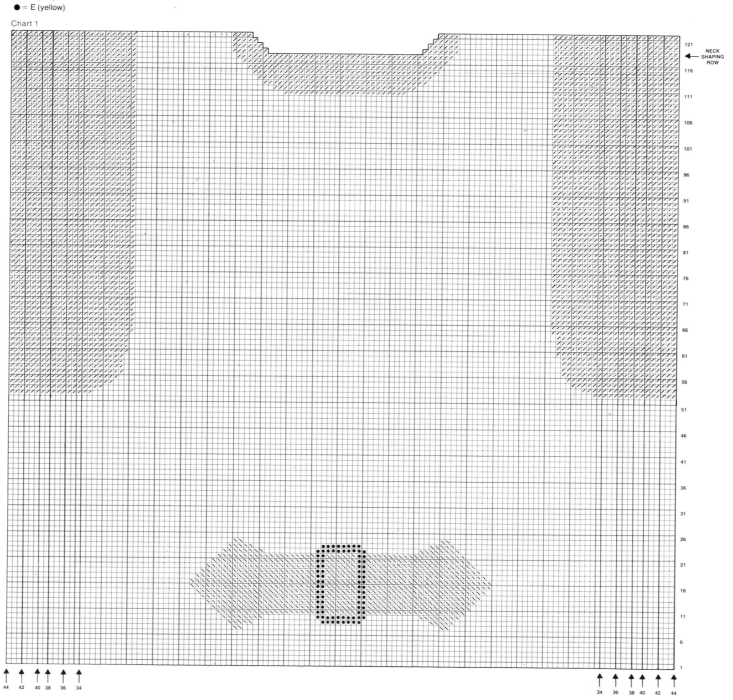

NECK
SHAPING
ROW

19

Chart 2

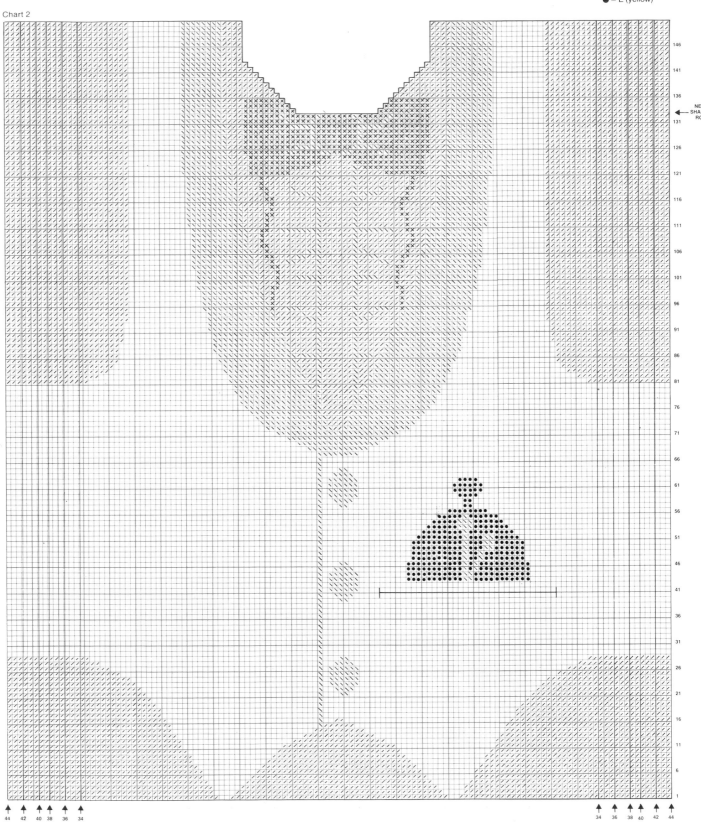

146

141

136

NECK
SHAPING
ROW

131

126

121

116

111

106

101

96

91

86

81

76

71

66

61

56

51

46

41

36

31

26

21

16

11

6

1

44 42 40 38 36 34

34 36 38 40 42 44

Sweet Dreams

MATERIALS

1(1: 2: 2) 100g balls of ARGYLL FLUFFY CHUNKY in pink, 1st contrast (A).
2 balls in mauve, main colour (B).
1 ball in brown, 2nd contrast (C).
Small amount of black yarn.
1 pair each of 4½mm. (No. 7) and 5½mm. (No. 5) knitting needles.
3 small black buttons or beads.
2 stitch holders.
The quantities of yarn given are based on average requirements and are therefore approximate.

MEASUREMENTS

To fit chest/bust: 66(71: 76: 81)cm. (26(28: 30: 32)in.)
Actual measurement: 69(74: 80: 86)cm. (27½(29½: 32: 34)in.)
Length from shoulder: 44(49: 54: 59)cm. (17¼(19¼: 21¼: 23¼)in.)
Sleeve length: 38(42: 44: 47) cm. (15(16½: 17½: 18½)in.)
Figures in brackets refer to the larger sizes. Where only one figure is given this refers to all sizes.

TENSION

14 sts. and 19 rows to 10cm. (4in.) on 5½mm. needles over st. st.

ABBREVIATIONS

K = knit; **P** = purl; **st.(s.)** = stitch(es); **st. st.** = stocking stitch; **patt.** = pattern; **foll.** = following; **inc.** = increase; **dec.** = decrease; **cont.** = continue; **RS** = right side; **WS** = wrong side; **rep.** = repeat; **rem.** = remaining; **B** = main colour; **A, C** = contrast colours; **mm.** = millimetres; **cm.** = centimetres; **in.** = inches.

INSTRUCTIONS

Back

With 4½mm. needles and A, cast on 40(42: 44: 46) sts. and work in K1, P1, rib for 14 rows.
Change to 5½mm. needles.
Increase row: K9(7: 5: 3), inc. in next st., *K2, inc. in next st., rep. from * to last 9(7: 5: 3) sts., K to end. (48(52: 56;

This dog obviously spends all day dreaming – he's bone idle! He is modelled by Sophie Lewis, Linda's eleven-year-old niece, who is as nice as she looks. (She must be nice because she laughed at my favourite doggie joke:
  'Doctor, doctor, I think I'm a dog!'
  'How long have you had this problem?'
  'Ever since I was a puppy.')

60)sts.)

Next row: P. **

Now starting with a K row, work straight in st. st. in A for 24(28: 32: 36) rows. Now change to B and cont. straight in st. st. until back measures 42(47: 52: 57)cm. (16½(18½: 20½: 22½)in.) from cast-on edge, ending with a WS row.

Shape back neck
Next row: K17(19: 21: 23)sts., turn and cont. on this first set of sts. only, placing rem. sts. on a stitch holder.
*** Dec. 1 st. at neck edge on next 3 rows.
Cast off rem. 14(16: 18: 20) sts. fairly loosely.
Return to rem. sts. and slip first 14 sts. onto stitch holder, with RS facing rejoin yarn to rem. sts. and K to end of row.
Now work as for first side from *** to end.

Front
Work as for back to **
Now starting with a K row, work straight in st. st. in A for 0(4: 8: 12) rows.

Place chart
1st row: (RS facing) K0(2: 4: 6)A, now work across the 34sts. from 1st row of **Chart 1**, K14(16: 18: 20)A.
The chart is now set.
Cont. to work from **Chart 1** until 52nd row has been worked. Now work in st. st. and B only until front measures 33(38: 43: 48)cm. (13(15: 17: 19)in.) from cast-on edge ending with a WS row. (NB. on smallest size **Chart 1** will still be being worked.)

Place chart
1st row (RS facing) K34(36: 38: 40)B, now work across the 13 sts. from 1st row of **Chart 2**, K1(3: 5: 7)B.
Cont. as set until the 6th row of **Chart 2** has been worked, thus ending with a WS row.

Shape front neck
Next row: K19(21: 23: 25)sts., turn and cont. on this first set of sts. only, placing rem. sts. on a stitch holder.
**** Dec. 1 st. at neck edge on every row until 14(16: 18: 20)sts. remain.
Now cont. straight in st. st. until front measures the same as back to cast-off shoulder edge, ending with a WS row.
Cast off all sts. fairly loosely.
Return to rem. sts. and slip first 10 sts. onto stitch holder. With RS facing rejoin yarn to rem. sts. and patt. to end

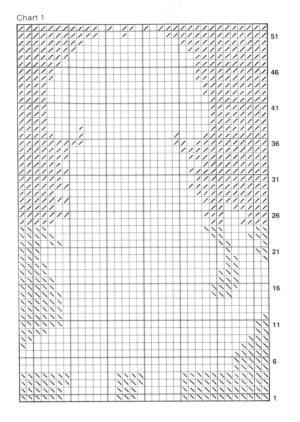

Chart 1

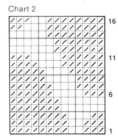

Chart 2

\\ = A (pink)
// = B = main colour (mauve)
□ = C (brown)

of row. (7th row of chart).
Now work as for first side from **** to end, keeping chart correct.

Sleeves
With 4½mm. needles and A, cast on 24 sts. and work in K1, P1, rib for 14 rows. Change to 5½mm. needles.
Increase row: *K1, inc. in next st., rep. from * to end. (36 sts.)
Now, starting with a P row, cont. in st. st. in A, inc. 1 st. at each end of every foll. 6th row until there are 46 sts. on the needle, then change to B and cont. to inc. as before until there are 48(50: 54: 56)sts. on the needle.
Now work straight in st. st. in B until sleeve measures 38(42: 44: 47)cm. (15(16½: 17½: 18½)in.) from cast-on edge, ending with a WS row.
Cast off all sts. fairly loosely.

Neckband
Join right shoulder seam.
With 4½mm. needles and B and RS facing, pick up and K12 sts. down left front neck, K10 sts. from stitch holder, pick up and K12 sts. up right front neck, K4 sts. down right back neck, K14 sts. from stitch holder, and finally pick up and K4 sts. up left back neck. (56 sts.)
Work in K1, P1, rib for 10 rows.
Cast off fairly loosely ribwise.

TO MAKE UP

Press according to ball band instructions.
Join left shoulder and neckband seam. Fold neckband in half to inside and slip stitch loosely in position. Measure and mark 18(19: 20: 21)cm. (7(7½: 8: 8½)in.) each side of shoulder seam and sew sleeves between these marks. Embroider face with black yarn and sew on beads for eyes and nose as in picture. Using a chain stitch and C embroider 'bubbles' as in picture. Join side and sleeve seams.

Noteworthy

Wherever she is – hovering in the heavens in her helicopter, sunning herself in the South Seas, prancing across the stage as a perfect pantomime principal boy – Anneka Rice always strikes the right note. Here she is again, doing just that for *Knitability*.

MATERIALS

7(7: 8: 8: 8: 9) 50g balls of MOHAIR yarn in main colour, red (A).
2 balls in 2nd colour, black (B).
1 pair each of 4½mm. (No. 7) and 5½mm. (No. 5) knitting needles.
2 stitch holders.

The quantities of yarn given are based on average requirements and are therefore approximate.

☐ = A = main colour (red)
╱ = B (black)

Chart 1

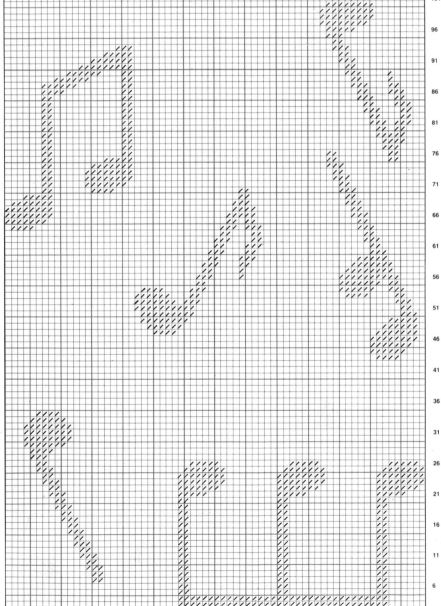

MEASUREMENTS

To fit bust/chest: 86(91: 96: 101: 107: 112)cm. (34(36: 38: 40: 42: 44)in.)
Actual measurement: 90(95: 100: 105: 110: 115)cm. (36(38: 40: 42: 44: 46)in.)
Length from shoulder: 64(67: 69: 72: 72: 72)cm. (25½(26½: 27½: 28½: 28½: 28½)in.)
Sleeve length: 48(48: 48: 51: 51: 51)cm. (19(19: 19: 20: 20: 20)in.)
Figures in brackets refer to the larger sizes. Where only one figure is given this refers to all sizes.

TENSION

16 sts. and 20 rows to 10cm. (4in.) on 5½mm. needles over st. st.

ABBREVIATIONS

K = knit; **P** = purl; **st.(s.)** = stitch(es); **st. st.** = stocking stitch; **foll.** = following; **inc.** = increase; **dec.** = decrease; **cont.** = continue; **RS** = right side; **WS** = wrong side; **rep.** = repeat; **patt.** = pattern; **rem.** = remaining; **A** = main colour; **B** = 2nd colour; **mm.** = millimetres; **cm.** = centimetres; **in.** = inches.

INSTRUCTIONS

Back
With 4½mm. needles and A, cast on 56(60: 64: 68: 72: 76)sts. and work in K1, P1, rib for 16 rows.
Change to 5½mm. needles.
Increase row: K5(7: 9: 3: 5: 7), inc. in next st., *K2(2: 2: 3: 3: 3), inc. in next st., rep. from * to last 5(7: 9: 4: 6: 8)sts., K to end of row. (72(76: 80: 84: 88: 92)sts.)
Next row: P.
Now starting with a K row work 4(6: 8: 10: 10: 10) rows straight in st. st. in A, thus ending with a WS row.
Place chart
Next row: K2(4: 6: 8: 10: 12)A, now work across the 68 sts. of 1st row of **Chart 1**, K2(4: 6: 8: 10: 12)A. **
The chart is now set. Cont. to follow chart until the 102 rows of chart have been worked.
Now work straight in st. st. in A until back measures 62(65: 67: 70: 70: 70)cm. (24½(25½: 26½: 27½: 27½: 27½)in.) from cast-on edge, ending with a WS row.
Shape back neck
Next row: K26(28: 30: 32: 34: 36)sts., turn and cont. on this first set of sts. only, placing rem. sts. on a stitch holder.
*** Dec. 1 st. at neck edge on next 3 rows.
Cast off rem. 23(25: 27: 29: 31: 33)sts. fairly loosely.
Return to rem. sts. and slip first 20 sts. onto stitch holder. With RS facing rejoin yarn to rem. sts. and K to end of row.
Now work as for first side from *** to end.

Front

Work as for back to **
The chart is now set. Cont. to follow chart until front measures 56(59: 61: 64: 64: 64)cm. (22(23: 24: 25: 25: 25)in.) from cast-on edge, ending with a WS row.

Shape front neck

Next row: Patt. 29(31: 33: 35: 37: 39)sts; turn and cont. on this first set of sts. only, placing rem. sts. on a stitch holder.

**** Keeping patt. correct, dec. 1 st. at neck edge on every row until 23(25: 27: 29: 31: 33)sts. remain.

When chart is complete, cont. straight in A until front measures the same as back to shoulder cast-off edge, ending with a WS row.

Cast off all sts. fairly loosely.

Return to rem. sts. and slip first 14 sts. onto stitch holder. With RS facing rejoin yarn to rem. sts. and patt. to end of row.

Now work as for first side from **** to end.

Sleeves

With 4½mm. needles and A, cast on 32 sts. and work in K1, P1, rib for 14 rows.
Change to 5½mm. needles.
Increase row: *K1, inc. in next st., rep. from * to end. (48 sts.)
Next row: P.
Now starting with a K row cont. in st. st. in A, **at the same time**, inc. 1 st. at each end of 7th row and then every foll. 6th row, and also work from 1st row of **chart 2**. Cont. to follow chart, working incs. as indicated until the 74 rows of chart are worked. Now cont. in A, and inc. as before, until there are 74 sts. on the needle.
Now work straight in st. st. until sleeve measures 48(48: 48: 51: 51: 51) cm. (19(19: 19: 20: 20: 20)in.) from cast-on edge, ending with a WS row.
Cast off all sts. fairly loosely.

Neckband

Join right shoulder seam.
With 4½mm. needles and A and RS facing, pick up and K14 sts. down left front neck, K14 sts. from stitch holder, pick up and K14 sts. up right front neck, K4 sts. down right back neck, K20 sts. from stitch holder and finally pick up and K4 sts. up left back neck. (70 sts.)
Work in K1, P1, rib for 10 rows.
Cast off fairly loosely ribwise.

Chart 2

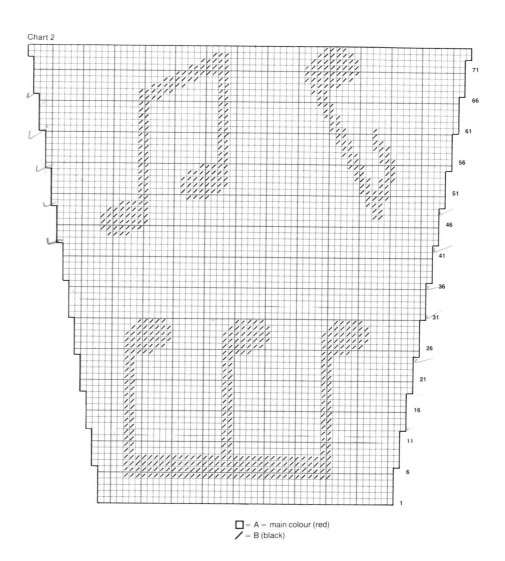

□ = A = main colour (red)
╱ = B (black)

TO MAKE UP

Press according to ball band instructions.
Join left shoulder and neckband seam. Fold neckband in half to inside and slip stitch loosely in position. Measure and mark 25cm. (10in.) each side of shoulder seam and sew sleeves between these marks.
Join side and sleeve seams.

Bear Necessity

'B'ear is beautiful.' That's my motto, which is why I love wearing this fabulous jumper. It's a must for every arctophile – that's what we Teddy Bear enthusiasts call ourselves when we want to sound grand – and I hope that includes you. For my money, there isn't a friendlier fun knit in the book.

MATERIALS

3(3: 3: 4: 4: 4) 50g balls of SIRDAR COUNTRY STYLE DK in 1st colour, mid-blue (A).
4 balls in 2nd colour, light blue (B).
2 balls in 3rd colour, yellow (C).
1 ball in 4th colour, cinnamon (D).
1 pair each of 3¼mm. (No. 10) and 4mm. (No. 8) knitting needles.
2 small buttons or beads for eyes.

2 stitch holders.

The quantities of yarn given are based on average requirements and are therefore approximate.

MEASUREMENTS

To fit chest/bust: 86(91: 96: 101: 107: 112)cm. (34(36: 38: 40: 42: 44)in.)
Actual measurement: 90(95: 100: 105: 110: 115)cm. 36:(38: 40: 42: 44: 46)in.)
Length from shoulder: 63(66: 69: 71: 71: 71)cm. (25(26: 27: 28: 28: 28)in.)
Sleeve length: 48(48: 48: 51: 51: 51)cm. (19(19: 19: 20: 20: 20)in.)
Figures in brackets refer to the larger sizes. Where only one figure is given this refers to all sizes.

TENSION

24 sts. and 30 rows to 10cm. (4in.) on 4mm. needles over st. st.

ABBREVIATIONS

K = knit; **P** = purl; **st.(s.)** = stitch(es); **st. st.** = stocking stitch; **foll.** = following; **inc.** = increase; **dec.** = decrease; **cont.** = continue; **RS** = right side; **WS** = wrong side; **rep.** = repeat; **rem.** = remaining; **DK** = double knitting; **A,B,C,D** = contrast colours; **mm.** = millimetres; **cm.** = centimetres, **in.** = inches.

Note

The outlines round the teddy's legs and chin, and its mouth, worked in D, may be embroidered or swiss-darned when work is complete rather than knitted, if preferred.

INSTRUCTIONS

Back

With 3¼mm. needles and A, cast on 90(96: 102: 106: 112: 118) sts. and work in K1, P1, rib for 20 rows.
Change to 4mm. needles.
Increase row: K2(5: 8: 5: 8: 11), inc. in next st., *K4, inc. in next st., rep from * to last 2(5: 8: 5: 8: 11)sts., K to end of row. (108(114:120:126:132:138)sts.)
Next row: P. **
Now starting with a K row work straight in st. st. in A for 26(30: 34: 38: 38: 38) rows, thus ending with a WS row.
Place chart
1st row: K9(12: 15: 18: 21: 24)A, work across the 90 sts. of 1st row of **Chart**

1, K9(12: 15: 18: 21: 24)A.
The chart is now set. Cont. to follow the chart until the 114 rows have been worked, thus ending with a WS row.
Now cont. straight in st. st. in B only until back measures 62(65: 68: 70: 70: 70)cm. (24½(25½: 26½: 27½: 27½: 27½)in.) from cast-on edge, ending with a WS row.
Shape back neck
Next row K39(42: 45: 46: 49: 52)sts., turn and cont. on this first set of sts. only, placing rem. sts. on a stitch holder.
*** Dec. 1st. at neck edge on next 3 rows.
Cast off rem. 36(39: 42: 43: 46: 49)sts. fairly loosely.
Return to rem. sts. and slip first 30(30: 30: 34: 34: 34)sts. onto a stitch holder. With RS facing rejoin yarn to rem. sts. and K to end of row.
Now work as for first side from *** to end.

Front
Work as for back to **
Now starting with a K row work straight in st. st. for 0(4: 8: 12: 12: 12) rows, thus ending with a WS row.
Place chart
1st row: K9(12: 15: 18: 21: 24)A, work across the 90 sts. of 1st row of **Chart 2**, K9(12: 15: 18: 21: 24)A.
The chart is now set. Cont. to follow the chart until the 140 rows have been worked, thus ending with a WS row.
Now work in st. st. in B only until front measures 56(59: 62: 64: 64: 64)cm. (22(23: 24: 25: 25: 25)in.) from cast-on edge, ending with a WS row.
Shape front neck
Next row: K46(49: 52: 54: 57: 60)sts., turn and cont. on this first set of sts. only, placing rem. sts. on a stitch holder.
**** Dec. 1 st. at neck edge on every row until 36(39: 42: 43: 46: 49)sts. remain.
Now cont. straight in st. st. until front measures the same as back to shoulder cast-off edge, ending with a WS row.
Cast off all sts. fairly loosely.
Return to rem. sts. and slip first 16(16: 16: 18: 18: 18)sts. onto stitch holder. With RS facing rejoin yarn to rem. sts. and K to end of row.
Now work as for first side from **** to end.

Sleeves
With 3¼mm. needles and A, cast on 48 sts. and work in K1, P1, rib for 20 rows.
Change to 4mm. needles.
Increase row: K8(8: 8: 2: 2: 2), inc. in next st., *K1, inc. in next st., rep from * to last 9(9: 9: 3: 3: 3)sts., K to end. (64(64: 64: 70: 70: 70)sts.)
Now starting with a P row cont. in st. st., in A, **at the same time**, inc. 1 st. at each end of every foll. 6th row until there are 76(76: 76: 82: 82: 82)sts. on the needle, ending with a WS row.
Now change to B and cont. in st. st. and inc. as before until there are 102(102: 102: 108: 108: 108)sts. on the needle. Now cont. straight in st. st. in B until sleeve measures 48(48: 48: 51: 51: 51)cm. (19(19: 19: 20: 20: 20)in.) from cast-on edge, ending with a WS row.
Cast off all sts. fairly loosely.

Neckband
Join right shoulder seam.
With 3¼mm. needles and B and RS facing, pick up and K23 sts. down left front neck, K16(16: 16: 18: 18: 18) sts. from stitch holder, pick up and K23 sts. up right front neck, K4 sts. down right back neck, K30(30: 30: 34: 34: 34) sts. from stitch holder and finally pick up and K4 sts. up left back neck. (100(100: 100: 106: 106: 106)sts.)
Work in K1, P1, rib for 12 rows.
Cast off fairly loosely ribwise.

TO MAKE UP

Press according to ball band instructions.
Join left shoulder and neckband seam. Fold neckband in half to inside and slip stitch loosely in position. Measure and mark 23(23: 23: 24: 24: 24)cm. (9(9: 9: 9½: 9½: 9½)in.) each side of shoulder seam and sew sleeves between these marks.
Sew beads or buttons in place for eyes, as in picture. Join side and sleeve seams.

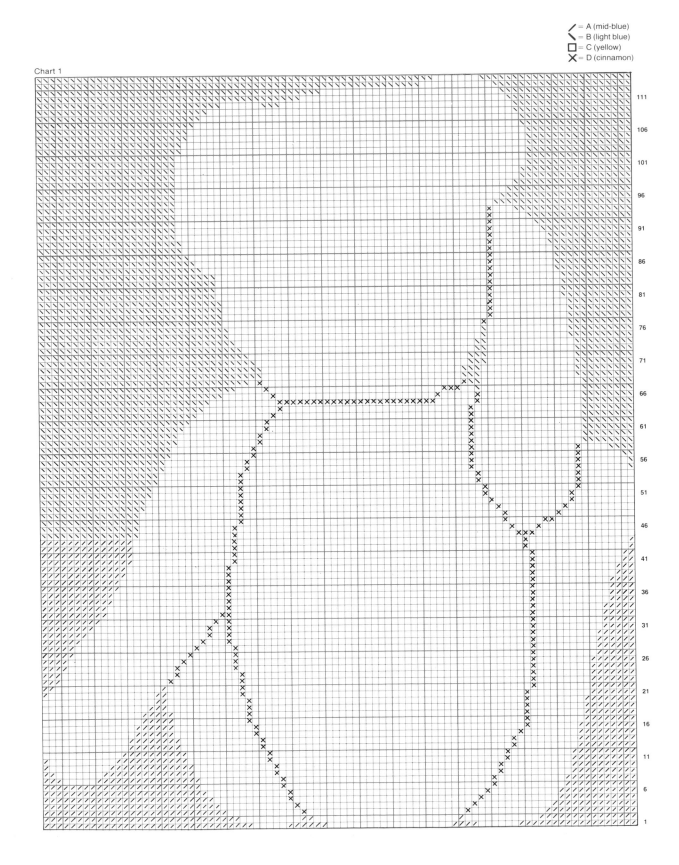

Chart 1

Chart 2

136

131

126

121

116

111

106

101

96

91

86

81

76

71

66

61

56

51

46

41

36

31

26

21

16

11

6

1

Baby Bear

The peacefully sleeping baby bear is worn by the baby of the Brandreth family, Aphra. It's quite wrong to call her the baby of the family when she's nine, but she's very sweetly forgiven her father for this unfortunate lapse. She knows it makes *me* feel younger.

MATERIALS

4 50g balls of PATONS DIPLOMA DK in main colour, light grey (A).
2 balls in each of 2 other colours, blue (B) and pink (C).
1 ball in each of 3 other colours, charcoal grey (D), white (E) and black (F).
1 pair each of 3¼mm. (No. 10) and 4mm. (No. 8) knitting needles.
2 stitch holders.
The quantities of yarn given are based on average requirements and are therefore approximate.

MEASUREMENTS

To fit chest: 56(61: 66)cm. (22(24: 26)in.)
Actual measurement: 60(66: 71)cm. (24(26: 28)in.)
Length from shoulder: 38(40: 43)cm. (15(16: 17)in.)
Sleeve length: 28(33: 38)cm. (11(13: 15)in.)
Figures in brackets refer to the larger sizes. Where only one figure is given this refers to all sizes.

TENSION

22 sts. and 30 rows to 10cm. (4in.) on 4mm. needles over st. st.

ABBREVIATIONS

K = knit; **P** = purl; **st.(s)** = stitch(es); **st. st.** = stocking stitch; **foll.** = following; **inc.** = increase; **dec.** = decrease; **cont.** = continue; **RS** = right side; **WS** = wrong side; **rep.** = repeat; **rem.** = remaining; **DK** = double knitting: **A** = main colour; **B,C,D,E,F** = contrast colours; **mm.** = millimetres; **cm.** = centimetres; **in.** = inches.
Note
The outlines round the bear's chin and legs, worked in A, and its features, worked in F, may be embroidered or swiss-darned when work is complete rather than knitted, if preferred.

INSTRUCTIONS

Back
With 3¼mm. needles and A, cast on 54(60: 66)sts and work in K1, P1, rib for

16 rows.
Change to 4mm. needles.
Increase row: K4(7: 10), inc. in next st, *K3, inc. in next st., rep. from * to last 5(8: 11) sts., K to end of row. (66(72: 78)sts.)
Next row: P. **
Now starting with a K row work in st. st. in the following stripe sequence:
Work 2 rows in B. Work 2 rows in C. Work 2 rows in A.
Rep. these 6 rows 7 times more. (48 stripe rows worked in all.)
Now cont. straight in st. st. in A only until back measures 37(39: 42)cm. (14½(15½: 16½)in.) from cast-on edge, ending with a WS row.
Shape back neck
Next row: K22(25: 28)sts., turn and cont. on this first set of sts. only, placing rem. sts. on a stitch holder.
*** Dec. 1 st. at neck edge on next 3 rows.
Cast off rem. 19(22:25) sts. fairly loosely.
Return to rem. sts. and slip first 22 sts. onto stitch holder. With RS facing rejoin yarn to rem. sts. and K to end of row.
Now work as for first side from *** to end.

Front
Work as for back to **
Now starting with a K row work in st. st. in the same stripe sequence as for back but work only 10 stripe rows, thus ending with 2 rows C.

Place chart
Next row: (RS facing) K3 (6:9)A, now work across the 60 sts. of 1st row from chart, K3(6:9)A.
Cont. as now set until the 60 rows of chart have been worked, working sts. either side of chart in correct stripe sequence.
Now cont. straight in st. st. in A only until front measures 32(34: 37)cm. (12½(13½: 14½)in.) from cast-on edge, ending with a WS row.
Shape front neck
Next row: K27(30: 33)sts., turn and cont. on this first set of sts. only, placing rem. sts. on a stitch holder.
**** Dec. 1 st. at neck edge on every row until 19(22: 25)sts. remain.
Now cont. straight in st. st. until front measures the same as back to shoulder cast-off edge, ending with a WS row.

Cast off all sts. fairly loosely.
Return to rem. sts. and slip first 12 sts. onto stitch holder. With RS facing rejoin yarn to rem. sts. and K to end of row.
Now work as for first side from **** to end.

Sleeves
With 3¼mm. needles and A, cast on 36 sts. and work in K1, P1, rib for 14 rows.
Change to 4mm. needles.
Increase row: *K1, inc. in next st., rep. from * to end. (54 sts.)
Next row: P.
Now starting with a K row work in st. st. and stripe sequence as for back, **at the same time,** inc. 1 st. at each end of 5th row and every foll. 6th row until there are 68(74: 80)sts. on the needle, working inc. sts. into the stripe sequence.
Now cont. straight in st. st. and stripes until sleeve measures 28(33: 38)cm. (11(13: 15)in.) from cast-on edge, ending with a WS row.
Cast off all sts. fairly loosely.

Neckband
Joint right shoulder seam.
With 3¼mm. needles and A and RS facing, pick up and K16 sts. down left front neck, K12 sts. from stitch holder, pick up and K16 sts. up right front neck, K4 sts. down right back neck, K22 sts. from stitch holder and finally pick up and K4 sts. up left back neck. (74 sts.)
Work in K1, P1, rib for 12 rows.
Cast off fairly loosely ribwise.

TO MAKE UP

Press according to ball band instructions.
Join left shoulder and neckband seam. Fold neckband in half to inside and slip stitch loosely in position.
Measure and mark 17(18: 19)cm (6½(7: 7½)in.) each side of shoulder seam and sew sleeves between these marks.
Join side and sleeve seams.

□ = A (light blue)   X = C (pink)   \ = E (white)
● = B (blue)   / = D (charcoal grey)   O = F (black)

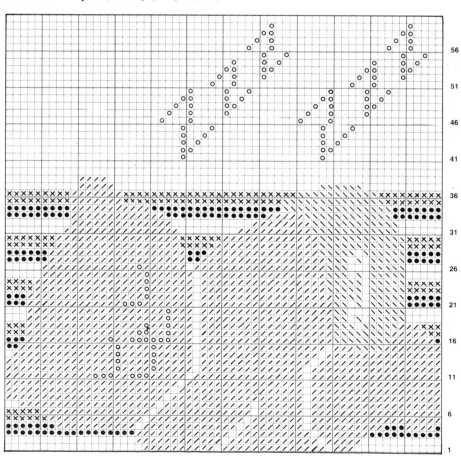

Peacock Plumage

When it comes to the birds let's face it: the peacock's a lot lovelier than the peahen. When it comes to the Brandreths, the reverse is true – and the proof is this picture of my matchless wife. I call her a bird of paradise in human form. She calls herself Michèle Brown.

MATERIALS

5(5: 6: 6: 6) 50g balls of DOUBLE KNITTING COTTON in main colour, jade green (A).
1 ball in each of 2 other colours, turquoise (B) and purple (C).
Small amount of rust (D).
1 pair each of 3¼mm. (No. 10) and 4mm. (No. 8) knitting needles.
84 round sew-on diamante beads.
20 tear-drop sew-on diamante beads.
2 stitch holders.
The quantities of yarn given are based on average requirements and are therefore approximate.

MEASUREMENTS

To fit bust: 86(91: 96: 101: 106)cm. (34(36: 38: 40: 42)in.)
Actual measurement: 90(96:100:106: 110)cm. (36(38½: 40: 42½: 44)in.)
Length from shoulder: 52cm. (20½ in.)
Figures in brackets refer to the larger sizes. Where only one figure is given this refers to all sizes.

TENSION

20 sts. and 26 rows to 10cm. (4in.) on 4mm. needles over st. st.

ABBREVIATIONS

K = knit; **P** = purl; **st.(s)** = stitch(es); **st. st.** = stocking stitch; **foll.** = following; **dec.** – decrease; **cont.** = continue; **RS** = right side; **WS** = wrong side; **patt.** = pattern; **beg.** = beginning; **rem.** = remaining; **alt.** = alternate; **A** = main colour; **B,C,D,** = contrast colours; **mm.** = millimetres; **cm.** = centimetres; **in.** = inches.

INSTRUCTIONS

Back
With 3¼mm. needles and A, cast on 90(96: 100: 106: 110)sts. and work in K1, P1, rib for 4 rows.
Change to 4mm. needles.
Place chart
Now starting with a K row work straight in st. st. working from 1st row of chart, working between appropriate lines for size required. (**NOTE**. Peacock shape should NOT be worked, but work feather which appears in bold outline on peacock.) Cont. as set until 70th row of chart has been worked, thus ending with a WS row.
Shape armholes
Cast off 5(7: 8: 10: 11) sts. at beg. of next 2 rows.
Keeping chart correct, dec. 1 st. at each end of next 8 rows, then at each end of next row and 3 foll. 4th rows. (56(58: 60: 62: 64)sts.)
Now cont. to follow chart until 110th row has been worked, thus ending with a WS row.
Shape back neck
Next row: (111th row of chart) Patt. 23(24:25:26:27)sts., turn and cont. on this first set of sts. only, placing rem. sts. on a stitch holder.
** Keeping chart correct, dec. 2 sts. loosely at neck edge on next 2 rows. Now dec. 1 st. at neck edge on next 5 rows. Now dec. 1 st. at neck edge on next row and 3 foll. alt. rows. (10(11:12: 13: 14)sts.)
Now work straight in st. st. for 5 rows, thus ending with a WS row (130th row of chart complete.)
Cast off all sts fairly loosely.
Return to rem. sts. and slip first 10 sts. onto stitch holder. With RS facing rejoin yarn to rem. sts. and patt. to end of row.
Now work as for first side from ** to end, keeping chart correct.

Front
Work as for back, but working peacock shape, NOT feather which is inside outline.

Neckband
Join right shoulder seam.
With 3¼mm. needles and A and RS facing, pick up and K23 sts. down left front neck, K10 sts. from stitch holder, pick up and K23 sts. up right front neck, K23 sts. down right back neck, K10 sts. from stitch holder and finally pick up and K23 sts. up left back neck. (112 sts.)
Work in K1, P1, rib for 4 rows.
Cast off fairly loosely ribwise.

Armbands (alike)
Join left shoulder and neckband seam.
With 3¼mm. needles and A and RS facing, pick up and K110(116: 120: 126: 130)sts. evenly all around armhole edge.
Work in K1, P1, rib for 4 rows.
Cast off fairly loosely ribwise.

TO MAKE UP

Press according to ball band instructions.
Sew on beads as in picture. Join side and armband seams.

□ = A = main colour (jade green)
╲ = B (turquoise)
╱ = C (purple)
● = D (rust)

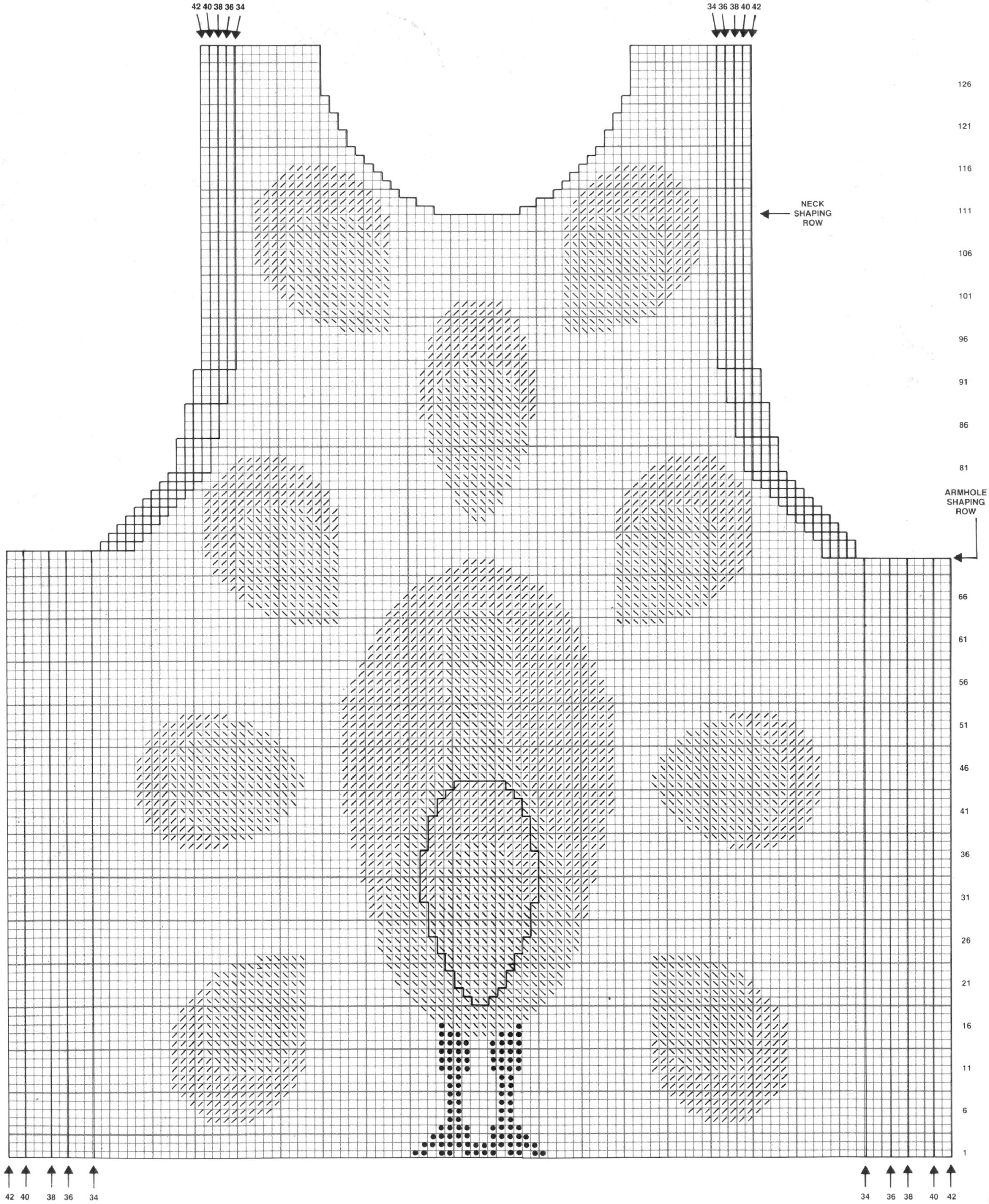

42 40 38 36 34

34 36 38 40 42

NECK
SHAPING
ROW

ARMHOLE
SHAPING
ROW

126

121

116

111

106

101

96

91

86

81

66

61

56

51

46

41

36

31

26

21

16

11

6

1

42 40   38 36   34

34   36 38   40 42

Pond Life

I first met the young Welsh boy soprano Aled Jones when he starred as Christopher Robin in a play I wrote with Julian Slade about the life and times of A.A. Milne. When I met him I knew he could sing like an angel. Soon I discovered he could act like Olivier as well. Now he turns out to be an ace model too, as you can see from the effortlessly stylish way he's sporting this lovely fun knit. (The frog's called Freddie, by the way, and he's a natural jumper.)

MATERIALS

8(8: 9) 25g balls of DOUBLE KNIT-TING in light blue, main colour (C).
2(2: 3) balls in brown, 1st contrast (A).
2 balls in royal blue, 2nd contrast (B).
1 ball in each of 3 other contrasting colours: green (D), yellow (E) and white (F).
Small amount of black.
1 pair each of 3¼mm. (No. 10) and 4mm. (No. 8) knitting needles.
4 small and 2 medium black buttons or beads for eyes.
2 stitch holders.
The quantities of yarn given are based on average requirements and are therefore approximate.

MEASUREMENTS

To fit chest/bust: 71(76: 81)cm. (28(30: 32)in.)
Actual measurement: 75(80: 86)cm. (30(32: 34)in.)
Length from shoulder: 49(54: 59)cm. (19¼(21¼: 23¼)in.)
Sleeve length: 42(45: 47)cm. (16¼(17¼: 18¼)in.)
Figures in brackets refer to the larger sizes. Where only one figure is given this refers to all sizes.

TENSION

22 sts. and 28 rows to 10cm. (4in.) on 4mm. needles over st. st.

ABBREVIATIONS

K = knit; **P** = purl; **st.(s.)** = stitch(es); **st. st.** = stocking stitch; **foll.** = following; **inc.** = increase; **dec.** = decrease; **cont.** = continue; **RS** = right side; **WS** = wrong side; **rep.** = repeat; **rem.** = remaining; **DK** = double knitting; **C** = main colour; **A,B,D,E,F** = contrast colours; **mm.** = millimetres; **cm.** = centimetres; **in.** = inches.

INSTRUCTIONS

Back

With 3¼mm. needles and A, cast on 70(76: 82)sts. and work in K1, P1, rib for 18 rows.
Change to 4mm. needles.
Increase row: K12(15: 18), inc. in next st., *K3, inc. in next st., rep. from * to last 13(16: 19)sts., K to end. (82(88:

94)sts.)
Next row: P.
Now, starting with a K row, work in st. st. for 0(6: 12) rows.**
Change to B and work a further 42 rows in st. st.
Change to A and work 14 more rows in st. st.
Now change to C and cont. straight in st. st. until back measures 47(52: 57)cm. (18½(20½: 22½)in.) from cast-on edge, ending with a WS row.

Shape back neck

Next row: K28(31: 34)sts., turn and cont. on this first set of sts. only, placing rem. sts. on a stitch holder.
*** Dec. 1 st. at neck edge on next 3 rows.
Cast off rem. 25(28: 31)sts. fairly loosely.
Return to rem. sts. and slip first 26 sts. onto stitch holder. With RS facing rejoin yarn to rem. sts. and K to end of row.
Now work as for first side from *** to end.

Front

Work as for back to **
Place chart
Now starting with the 1st row, work in st. st. from **Chart 1**, working between appropriate lines for size required.
Cont. as set until the 100 rows of chart have been worked.
Now cont. in C and work straight in st. st. until front measures 42(47: 52)cm (16½(18½: 20½)in) from cast-on edge, ending with a WS row.

Shape front neck

Next row: K34 (37: 40)sts., turn and cont. on this first set of sts. only, placing rem. sts. on a stitch holder.
**** Dec. 1 st. at neck edge on every row until 25(28: 31)sts. remain.
Now cont. straight in st. st. until front measures the same as back to cast-off shoulder edge, ending with a WS row.
Cast off all sts. fairly loosely.
Return to rem. sts. and slip first 14 sts. onto stitch holder, with RS facing rejoin yarn to rem. sts. and K to end of row.
Now work as for first side from **** to end.

Sun Sleeve

With 3¼mm. needles and C, cast on 40 sts. and work in K1, P1, rib for 18 rows.
Change to 4mm. needles.
Increase row: K6, inc. in next st, *K1,

inc. in next st., rep. from * to last 7 sts., K to end. (54 sts.)
Now starting with a P row, work in st. st., inc. 1 st. at each end of every foll. 6th row until there are 74(76: 78)sts. on the needle, ending with a WS row. //

Place chart

Next row: K27(28: 29)C, work across the 20 sts from 1st row of **Chart 2**, then K27(28: 29)C. Complete the 24 rows of chart, **at the same time**, cont. to inc. as before until there are 80(84: 88)sts. on the needle. When chart is complete, cont. in C only.
Now cont. straight in st. st. until sleeve measures 42(45: 47)cm. (16½(17½: 18½)in.) from cast-on edge, ending with a WS row.
Cast off all sts. fairly loosely.

Cloud Sleeve

Work as for sun sleeve to //.
Place chart
Next row: K12(13: 14)C, work across the 50 sts. from 1st row of **Chart 3**, K12(13: 14)C.
Complete the 30 rows of chart, and finish as for sun sleeve.

Neckband

Join right shoulder seam.
With 3¼mm. needles and C and RS facing, pick up and K18 sts. down left front neck, K14 sts. from stitch holder, pick up and K18 sts. up right front neck, K4 sts. down right back neck, K26 sts. from stitch holder, and finally pick up and K4 sts. up left back neck. (84 sts.)
Work in K1, P1, rib for 12 rows.
Cast off fairly loosely ribwise.

TO MAKE UP

Press according to ball band instructions.
Join left shoulder and neckband seam. Fold neckband in half to inside and slip stitch loosely in position. Measure and mark 19(20: 22)cm. (7½(8: 8½)in.) each side of shoulder seam and sew sleeves between these marks.
Sew small beads or buttons on fish and dragonfly for eyes and medium beads or buttons for frog's eyes. Using a chain stitch and E embroider sun's rays and with A the bulrush stalks as in picture. With black yarn embroider the frog's face.
Join side and sleeve seams.

Chart 1

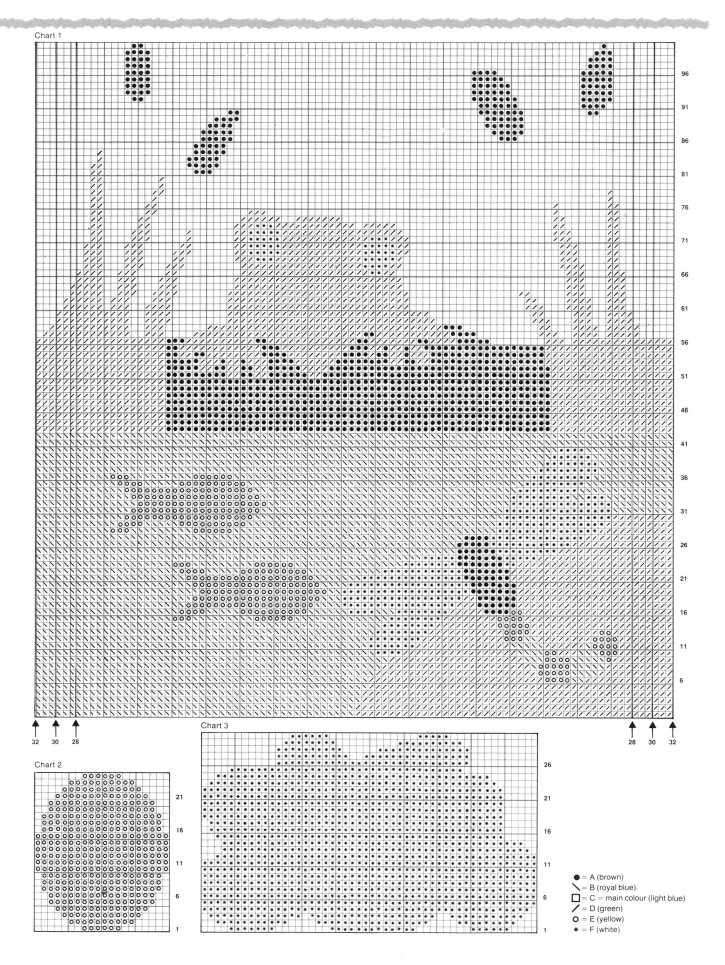

Chart 2

Chart 3

● = A (brown)
＼ = B (royal blue)·
□ = C = main colour (light blue)
／ = D (green)
O = E (yellow)
✱ = F (white)

Inter-City

When I told Linda's nephew George Lewis the joke about the station announcer who said over the loudspeaker, 'The train now arriving at platform six, seven, eight, nine and ten is coming in sideways,' he *groaned*! Apparently he'd heard it before – but then he is seven years old. He's also a railway enthusiast and thinks the train on this jumper is one of the nicest he's spotted.

MATERIALS

3(3: 3) 25g balls of DOUBLE KNIT-TING yarn in 1st colour, green (A).
4(5: 5) balls in 2nd colour, pale blue (B).
1 ball in each of 5 other colours, silver grey (C), charcoal grey (D), yellow (E), royal blue (F) and white (G).
1 pair each of 3¼mm. (No. 10) and 4mm. (No. 8) knitting needles.
2 small black beads or buttons.
14 small square or 7 oblong black beads or buttons.
2 stitch holders.
The quantities of yarn given are based on average requirements and are therefore approximate.

MEASUREMENTS

To fit chest: 56(61: 66)cm. (22(24: 26)in.)
Actual measurement: 60(66: 71)cm. (24(26: 28)in.)
Length from shoulder: 39(41: 44)cm. (15(16: 17)in.)
Sleeve length: 28(33: 38)cm. (11(13: 15)in.)
Figures in brackets refer to the larger sizes. Where only one figure is given this refers to all sizes.

TENSION

22 sts. and 28 rows to 10cm.(4in.) on 4mm. needles over st. st.

ABBREVIATIONS

K = knit; **P** = purl; **st.(s)** = stitch(es); **st. st.** = stocking stitch; **foll.** = following; **inc.** = increase; **dec.** = decrease; **cont.** = continue; **RS** = right side; **WS** = wrong side; **rep.** = repeat; **rem.** = remaining; **A,B,C,D,E,F,G** = contrast colours; **mm.** = millimetres; **cm.** = centimetres; **in.** = inches.

Note
The vertical and horizontal lines on the front of the train, worked in C, may be embroidered or swiss-darned when work is complete rather than knitted, if preferred.

INSTRUCTIONS

Back
With 3¼mm. needles and A, cast on 54(60: 66)sts., and work in K1, P1, rib for 18 rows.

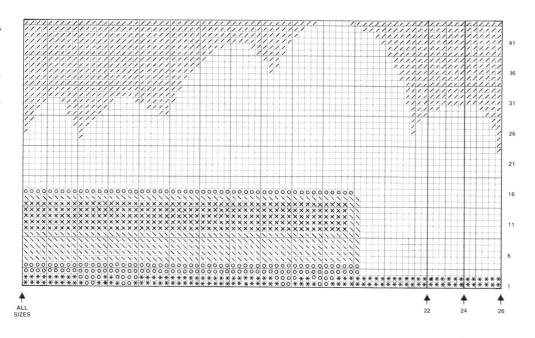

□ = A (green)
╱ = B (pale blue)
✳ = C (silver grey)
O = D (charcoal grey)
● = E (yellow)
╲ = F (royal blue)
X = G (white)

Chart 2

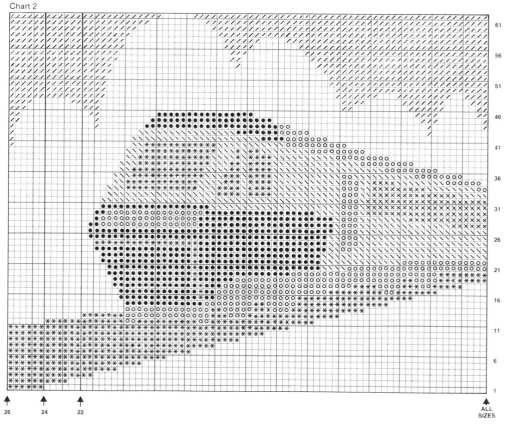

Change to 4mm. needles.

Increase row: K4(7: 10), inc. in next st., *K3, inc. in next st., rep. from * to last 5(8: 11)sts., K to end of row. (66(72: 78)sts.)

Next row: P. **

Now starting with a K row work 20(26: 32) rows straight in st. st. in A, thus ending with a WS row.

Place chart

Starting with the 1st row work in st. st. from **Chart 1**, working between appropriate lines for size required. Cont. as set until the 44 rows of chart have been worked.

Now cont. straight in st. st. in B until back measures 37(39: 42)cm. (14½(15¼: 16½)in.) from cast-on edge, ending with a WS row.

Shape back neck

Next row: K22(25: 28)sts., turn and cont. on this first set of sts. only, placing rem. sts. on a stitch holder.

*** Dec. 1 st. at neck edge on next 3 rows.

Cast off rem. 19(22: 25)sts. fairly loosely.

Return to rem. sts. and slip first 22 sts. onto stitch holder. With RS facing rejoin yarn to rem. sts. and K to end of row.

Now work as for first side from *** to end.

Front

Work as for back to **

Now starting with a K row work 2(8: 14) rows straight in st. st. in A, thus ending with a WS row.

Place chart

Starting with the 1st row work in st. st. from **Chart 2**, working between appropriate lines for size required. Cont. as set until the 62 rows of chart have been worked.

Now work straight in st. st. in B until front measures 32(34: 37)cm. (12½(13½: 14½)in.) from cast-on edge, ending with a WS row.

Shape front neck

Next row: K27(30: 33)sts., turn and cont. on this first set of sts. only, placing rem. sts. on a stitch holder.

**** Dec. 1 st. at neck edge on every row until 19(22: 25) sts. remain.

Now cont. straight until front measures the same as back to shoulder cast-off edge, ending with a WS row.

Cast off all sts. fairly loosely.

Return to rem. sts. and slip first 12 sts. onto stitch holder. With RS facing rejoin yarn to rem. sts. and K to end of row.

Now work as for first side from **** to end.

Sleeves

With 3¼mm. needles and B, cast on 36 sts. and work in K1, P1, rib for 18 rows. Change to 4mm. needles.

Increase row: *K1, inc. in next st., rep. from * to end. (54 sts.)

Now starting with a P row work in st. st. in B, **at the same time,** inc. 1 st. at each end of every foll. 6th row until there are 66(72: 78)sts. on the needle.

Now work straight in st. st. until sleeve measures 28(33: 38)cm. (11(13: 15)in.) from cast-on edge, ending with a WS row.

Cast off all sts. fairly loosely.

Neckband

Join right shoulder seam.

With 3¼mm. needles and B and RS facing, pick up and K17 sts. down left front neck, K12 sts. from stitch holder, pick up and K17 sts. up right front neck, K4 sts. down right back neck, K22 sts. from stitch holder and finally pick up and K4 sts. up left back neck. (76 sts.)

Work in K1, P1, rib for 12 rows.

Cast off fairly loosely ribwise.

TO MAKE UP

Press according to ball band instructions.

Join left shoulder and neckband seam. Fold neckband in half to inside and slip stitch loosely in position. Measure and mark 17(18: 19)cm. 6½(7: 7½)in. each side of shoulder seam and sew sleeves between these marks. Using G and a small daisy stitch, embroider logo on side of train as in picture. Sew small beads or buttons for headlights in place. Sew square or oblong beads or buttons in place for windows. Join side and sleeve seams.

Lovebirds

MATERIALS

7(8: 8) 25g balls of DOUBLE KNIT-
TING in blue, main colour (A).
1 25g ball in each of 5 contrasting
colours, light green (B), pink (C), emerald (D), grey (F) and brown (G).
Small amount of white (E).
1 pair each of 3¼mm. (No. 10) and
4mm. (No. 8) knitting needles.
2 small buttons or beads for eyes.
2 stitch holders.
*The quantities of yarn given are based
on average requirements and are
therefore approximate.*

MEASUREMENTS

To fit chest: 56(61: 66)cm. (22(24:
26)in.)
Actual measurement: 60(66: 71)cm.
(24(26: 28)in.)
Length from shoulder: 39(41: 44)cm.
(15¼(16¼: 17¼)in.)
Sleeve length: 28(33: 38)cm. (11(13:
15)in.)
Figures in brackets refer to the larger
sizes. Where only one figure is given
this refers to all sizes.

TENSION

22 sts. and 28 rows to 10cm. (4in.) on
4mm. needles over st. st.

ABBREVIATIONS

K = knit; **P** = purl; **st.(s)** = stitch(es); **st.
st.** = stocking stitch; **patt.** = pattern;
foll. = following; **inc.** = increase; **dec.**
= decrease; **cont.** = continue; **RS** =
right side; **WS** = wrong side; **rep.** =
repeat; **rem.** = remaining; **DK** = double
knitting; **A** = main colour; **B,C,D,
E,F,G,** = contrast colours; **mm.** = millimetres; **cm.** = centimetres; **in.** =
inches.

INSTRUCTIONS

Back

With 3¼mm. needles and A, cast on
54(60: 66)sts. and work in K1, P1, rib for
18 rows.
Change to 4mm. needles.
Increase row. K4(7: 10), inc. in next st.,
*K3, inc. in next st., rep. from * to last

T his is my ten-year-old daughter Saethryd Brandreth,
who has an unusual name because she's an unusual
girl. She also has an eye for the best in parrot-fashion
which is why she likes this parakeet jumper as much as I
do.

5(8: 11) sts. K to end. (66(72: 78)sts.)
Next row: P. **
Now starting with a K row, cont.
straight in st. st. until back measures
37(39: 42)cm. (14½(15½: 16½)in.)
from cast-on edge, ending with a WS
row.

Shape back neck
Next row: K22(25: 28)sts., turn and
cont. on this first set of sts. only, placing
rem. sts. on a stitch holder.
*** Dec. 1 st. at neck edge on next 3
rows.
Cast off rem. 19(22: 25)sts. fairly
loosely.
Return to rem. sts. and slip first 22 sts.
onto stitch holder, with RS facing rejoin
yarn to rem. sts. and K to end of row.
Now work as for first side from *** to
end.

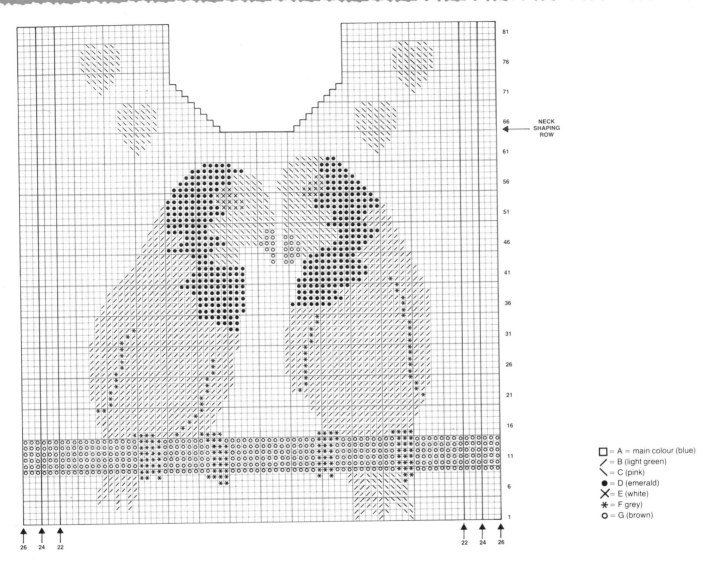

□ = A	= main colour (blue)
╱ = B	(light green)
╲ = C	(pink)
● = D	(emerald)
✕ = E	(white)
✱ = F	(grey)
○ = G	(brown)

NECK SHAPING ROW ←

Front

Work as for back to **
Starting with a K row, work straight in st. st. for 8(14: 22) rows.

Place chart

Now starting with the 1st row work from chart, working between appropriate lines for size required.
Cont. working from chart as set until the 64th row has been worked, thus ending with a WS row.

Shape front neck

Next row: (65th row of chart) Patt. 27(30: 33)sts., turn and cont. on this first set of sts. only, placing rem. sts. on a stitch holder.
**** Keeping chart correct, dec. 1 st. at neck edge on every row until 19(22: 25)sts. remain. Cont. straight until front measures the same as back to cast-off shoulder edge, ending with a WS row.
Cast off all sts. fairly loosely.

Return to rem. sts. and slip first 12 sts. onto stitch holder. With RS facing rejoin yarn to rem. sts. and patt. to end of row.
Now work as for first side from **** to end.

Sleeves

With 3¼mm. needles and A, cast on 36 sts. and work in K1, P1, rib for 18 rows.
Change to 4 mm. needles.
Increase row: *K1, inc. in next st., rep. from * to end. (54 sts.)
Starting with a P row cont. in st. st., inc. 1 st. at each end of every foll. 6th row until there are 66(72: 78)sts. on the needle.
Now cont. straight in st. st. until sleeve measures 28(33: 38)cm. (11(13: 15)in.) from cast-on edge, ending with a WS row.
Cast off all sts. fairly loosely.

Neckband

Join right shoulder seam.
With 3¼mm. needles and A and RS facing, pick up and K17 sts. down left front neck, K12sts. from stitch holder, pick up and K17 sts. up right front neck, K4 sts. down right back neck, K22 sts. from stitch holder, and finally pick up and K4 sts. up left back neck. (76 sts.)
Work in K1, P1, rib for 12 rows.
Cast off fairly loosely ribwise.

TO MAKE UP

Press according to ball band instructions.
Join left shoulder and neckband seam. Fold neckband in half to inside and slip stitch loosely in position. Measure and mark 17(18: 19)cm. (6½(7: 7½)in.) each side of shoulder seam and sew sleeves between these marks. Join side and sleeve seams. Sew on beads for eyes as in picture.

Horse Play

MATERIALS

4 25g balls of DOUBLE KNITTING yarn in 1st colour, charcoal grey (A). 10(11: 11) balls in 2nd colour, red (B). 1 ball in 3rd colour, silver grey (C).
1 pair each of 3¼mm. (No. 10) and 4mm. (No. 8) knitting needles.
4(4: 5) buttons.
13 small black beads.
1 medium size crochet hook.
3 stitch holders.
The quantities of yarn given are based on average requirements and are therefore approximate.

MEASUREMENTS

To fit chest/bust: 71(76: 81)cm. (28(30: 32)in.)
Actual measurement: 77(82: 88)cm. (30¾(32¾: 34¾)in.)
Length from shoulder: 48(53: 58)cm. (19(21: 23)in.)
Sleeve length: 42(44: 47)cm. (16½(17½: 18½)in.)
Figures in brackets refer to the larger sizes. Where only one figure is given this refers to all sizes.

TENSION

22 sts. and 28 rows to 10cm. (4in.) on 4mm. needles over st. st.

ABBREVIATIONS

K = knit; **P** = purl; **st.(s.)** = stitch(es); **tog.** = together; **alt.** = alternate; **st. st.** = stocking stitch; **patt.** = pattern; **foll.** = following; **inc.** = increase; **dec.** = decrease; **cont.** = continue; **RS** = right side; **WS** = wrong side; **rep.** = repeat; **rem.** = remaining; **patt. 2 tog.** = insert needle as though to knit next 2 sts. together then work a knit and a purl st. into them without slipping sts. off nee-

L ynsey de Paul is a brilliant actress, a superb song-writer and a fabulous friend. She also loves animals, but unfortunately there wasn't a horse to hand when she modelled this pony-lover's cardigan, so she had to sit on a sheep. Baaa!

dle until both sts. have been worked;
A,B,C = contrast colours; **mm.** = millimetres; **cm.** = centimetres; **in.** = inches.

Note

The lines round the pony's head and legs, worked in A, may be embroidered or swiss-darned when work is complete rather than knitted, if preferred.

INSTRUCTIONS

Back

With 3¼mm. needles and A, cast on 70(76:82)sts. and work in K1, P1, rib for 18 rows.

Change to 4mm. needles and B.

Increase row: K7(10: 13), inc, in next st.,*K4, inc. in next st., rep. from* to last 7(10: 13)sts., K to end of row. (82(88: 94)sts.)

Next row: P.

Now starting with a K row work 0(6:14) rows straight in st. st. in B, thus ending with a WS row.

Place chart

1st row: K13(16: 19)B, work across the 56 sts. from 1st row of **Chart 1**, K13(16: 19)B.

The chart is now set. Cont. to follow chart until the 70 rows have been worked, thus ending with a WS row.

Starting with a K row work 0(8: 14) rows in st. st.

Now work in pattern in B as follows:

1st row: (RS facing) K20(23: 26), patt. 2 tog., K38, patt. 2 tog; K20(23: 26).

Next and all alt. rows: P.

3rd row: K18(21: 24), (patt. 2 tog.) 3 times, K34, (patt. 2 tog.) 3 times, K18(21: 24).

5th row: K16(19: 22), (patt. 2 tog.) 5 times, K30, (patt. 2 tog.) 5 times, K16(19: 22).

7th row: K14(17: 20), (patt. 2 tog.) 7 times, K26, (patt. 2 tog.) 7 times, K14(17: 20).

Cont. in this way until complete row is patterned.

Now cont. straight in patt. as set until back measures 47(52: 57)cm. (18½(20½: 22½)in.) from cast-on edge, ending with a WS row.

Shape back neck

Next row: Patt. 28(31:34)sts., turn and cont. on this first set of sts. only, placing rem. sts. on a stitch holder.

** Keeping patt. correct, dec. 1 st. at neck edge on next 3 rows.

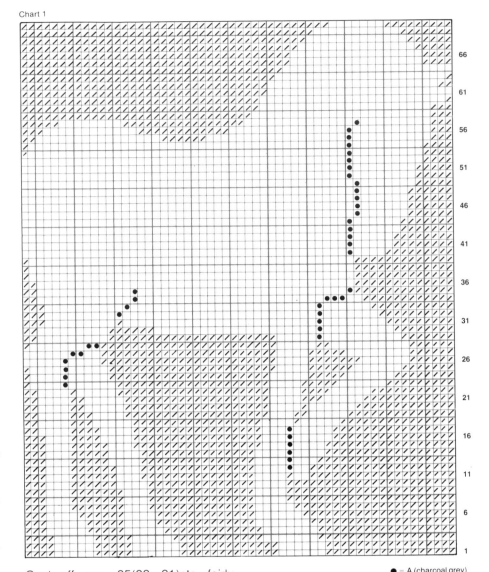

Chart 1

● = A (charcoal grey)
╱ = B (red)
□ = C (silver grey)

Cast off rem. 25(28: 31)sts. fairly loosely.

Return to rem. sts. and slip first 26 sts. onto stitch holder. With RS facing rejoin yarn to rem. sts. and patt. to end of row.

Now work as for first side from ** to end.

Pocket Lining (make 2)

With 4mm. needles and B, cast on 26 sts. and starting with a K row work straight in st. st. for 34 rows, thus ending with a WS row.

Leave sts. on a stitch holder.

Left Front

With 3¼mm. needles and A, cast on 35(38:41)sts. and work in K1, P1, rib for 18 rows.

Change to 4mm. needles and B.

Increase row: K7(10: 13), inc. in next st.,*K4, inc. in next st., rep. from* to last 2 sts, K to end of row. (41(44: 47)sts.)

Next row: P.

Place chart

1st row: K5(8: 11)B, work across the 26 sts. from 1st row of **Chart 2**, K10B.

The chart is now set. Cont. to follow chart until the 34 rows have been worked, thus ending with a WS row.

Place pocket

Next row: K5(8: 11), place next 26 sts. onto stitch holder, and then with RS facing, K across the 26 sts. from first pocket lining, K10.

Next row: P across all sts.

Now starting with a K row work 8(22: 36) rows in st. st.

Shape front neck

Next row: Dec. 1 st. at end (neck edge)

44

on next row and at this edge on every foll. 4th row until 34(37: 40)sts. remain, ending with a WS row.

Now work in pattern as follows:

1st row: K20(23: 26), patt. 2 tog., K12.

Next and all alt. rows: P.

3rd row: K18(21: 24), (patt. 2 tog.) 3 times, K8, K2 tog. (for neck shaping). Cont. in patt. as for back until all row is patterned and cont. to dec. 1 st. at neck edge on every foll. 4th row until 25(28: 31)sts. remain.

Now cont. straight in patt. as set until front measures the same as back to cast-off shoulder edge, ending with a WS row.

Cast off all sts. fairly loosely.

Right Front

Work as for left front but reverse increase row, pocket placing, all pattern and shaping.

Pocket Welt (alike)

With 3¼mm. needles and A and RS facing, pick up the 26 sts. from stitch holder and work in K1, P1, rib for 6 rows. Cast off fairly loosely ribwise.

Sleeves

With 3¼mm. needles and A, cast on 36 sts. and work in K1, P1, rib for 18 rows. Change to 4mm. needles and B.

Increase row: *K1, inc. in next st., rep. from * to end. (54 sts.)

Now starting with a P row work in st. st. in B, **at the same time**, inc. 1 st. at each end of every foll. 6th row until there are 80(84: 88)sts. on the needle.

Now work straight in st. st. until sleeve measures 42(44: 47)cm. (16½(17½: 18½)in.) from cast-on edge, ending with a WS row.

Cast off all sts. fairly loosely.

Front Bands and Collar

With 3¼mm. needles and A, cast on 9 sts. and work in rib as follows:

1st row: (RS facing) K1, *P1, K1, rep. from * to end.

2nd row: P1, *K1, P1, rep. from * to end.

**Next row:* (Buttonhole row) K1, P1, K1, P1, cast off 2 sts, K1, P1, K1.

Next row: Rib casting on 2 sts. over those cast off on previous row.

Rib a further 16(20: 18) rows.*

Now rep from * to * until 3(3: 4) buttonholes in all have been worked, then rep. 2 buttonhole rows once more, thus ending with a WS row. (4(4: 5) buttonholes worked in all.)

Shape collar

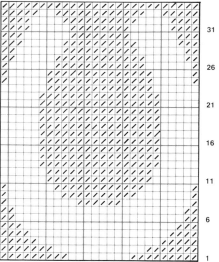

Chart 2

31
26
21
16
11
6
1

● = A (charcoal grey)
╱ = B (red)
□ = C (silver grey)

Inc. 1 st. at END of next row and at this edge on every foll. alt. row until there are 30 sts. on the needle, working inc. sts. into the rib.

Now work straight in rib until collar, when slightly stretched, fits neatly to centre back of neck. Mark this point with a contrast coloured thread.

Now work collar shaping in reverse and front band, but omit all buttonholes.

TO MAKE UP

Press according to ball band instructions. Sew both shoulder seams. Measure and mark 20(21: 22)cm. (7½(8: 8½)in.) each side of shoulder seam and sew sleeves between these marks.

Sew 6 beads on each horseshoe and 1 bead for eye of pony. Sew pocket linings neatly in position on wrong side and catch stitch pocket welts neatly at sides. Lay front bands and collar on right side of fronts, overlapping edges and pin evenly around neck, then using A and a small running stitch sew through edge stitch of band and fronts all around neckline.

Cut 20cm. (8in.) lengths in A then using 2 lengths and a crochet hook, work fringe across front and back yokes as shown in picture.

For tail, cut ten 25cm. (10in.) lengths in A. Tie around centre and sew in place. Work a short fringe for mane.

Trim all fringes evenly. Join side and sleeve seams. Sew on buttons to correspond with buttonholes.

Fisherman's Dream

When it comes to high fashion, this fellow's never out of plaice! Actor, dancer, host-with-the-most, yes it's a fellow with flair: it's Lionel Blair!

MATERIALS

1(2: 2: 2: 2: 2) 50g ball(s) of HAYFIELD GRAMPIAN DK in 1st colour, green (A).
1(1: 1: 2: 2: 2) ball(s) in 2nd colour, denim blue, (B).
5(5: 5: 6: 6: 6) balls in 3rd colour, light blue (C).
1 ball in each of 4 other colours, olive green (D), camel (E), brown (F) and grey (H).
Small amount of pink (G) and white (J).
1 pair each of 3¼mm. (No. 10) and 4mm. (No. 8) knitting needles.
3 small black beads or buttons for eyes; 3 fish beads; 1 brown button.
2 stitch holders.
The quantities of yarn given are based on average requirements and are therefore approximate.

MEASUREMENTS

To fit bust/chest: 86(91: 96: 101: 107: 112)cm. (34(36: 38: 40: 42: 44)in.)
Actual measurement: 91(97: 102: 106: 111: 116)cm. (36(38½: 40¾: 42: 44¼: 46½)in.)
Length from shoulder: 64(67: 69: 72: 72: 72)cm. (25(26: 27: 28: 28: 28)in.)
Sleeve length: 48(48: 48: 51: 51: 51)cm. (19(19: 19: 20: 20: 20)in.)
Figures in brackets refer to the larger sizes. Where only one figure is given this refers to all sizes.

TENSION

22 sts. and 28 rows to 10cm. (4in.) on 4mm. needles over st. st.

ABBREVIATIONS

K = knit; **P** = purl; **st.(s.)** = stitch(es); **st. st.** = stocking stitch; **foll.** = following; **inc.** = increase; **dec.** = decrease; **cont.** = continue; **RS** = right side; **WS** = wrong side; **rep.** = repeat; **rem.** = remaining; **DK** = double knitting; **A,B,C,D,E,F,G,H,J** = contrast colours; **mm.** = millimetres; **cm.** = centimetres; **in.** = inches.

INSTRUCTIONS

Back

With 3¼mm. needles and A, cast on 82(88: 94: 98: 104: 110)sts. and work in K1, P1, rib for 18 rows.
Change to 4mm. needles.
Increase row: K6(9: 12: 14: 17: 20), inc. in next st., *K3, inc. in next st., rep. from * to last 7(10: 13: 15: 18: 21)sts., K to end of row. (100(106: 112: 116: 122: 128)sts.)
Next row: P. **
Now starting with a K row work straight in st. st. in A for 28(32: 36: 40: 40: 40) rows, thus ending with a WS row.
Change to B and work straight in st. st. for a further 40 rows, thus ending with a WS row.
Now change to C and cont. straight in st. st. until back measures 62(65: 67: 70: 70: 70)cm. (24½(25½: 26½: 27½: 27½: 27½)in.) from cast-on edge, ending with a WS row.
Shape back neck
Next row: K35(38: 41: 43: 46: 49)sts., turn and cont. on this first set of sts. only, placing rem. sts. on a stitch holder.
***Dec. 1 st. at neck edge on next 3 rows.
Cast off rem. 32(35: 38: 40: 43: 46)sts. fairly loosely.
Return to rem. sts. and slip first 30 sts. onto stitch holder. With RS facing rejoin yarn to rem. sts. and K to end of row.
Now work as for first side from *** to end.

Front

Work as for back to **
Now starting with a K row work straight in st. st. in A for 0(4: 8: 12: 12: 12) rows, thus ending with a WS row.
Place chart
Now starting with the 1st row work in st. st. from chart, working between appropriate lines for size required. Cont. straight as set until the 134 rows of chart have been worked.
Now cont. in C only, and cont. straight in st. st. until front measures 56(59: 61: 64: 64: 64)cm. (22(23: 24: 25: 25: 25)in.) from cast-on edge, ending with a WS row.
Shape front neck
Next row: K42(45: 48: 50: 53: 56)sts., turn and cont. on this first set of sts. only, placing rem. sts. on a stitch holder.
**** Dec. 1 st. at neck edge on every row until 32(35: 38: 40: 43: 46)sts. remain.
Now cont. straight until front measures the same as back to shoulder cast-off edge, ending with a WS row.
Cast off all sts. fairly loosely.
Return to rem. sts. and slip first 16 sts. onto stitch holder. With RS facing rejoin yarn to rem. sts. and K to end of row.
Now work as for first side from **** to end.

Sleeves

With 3¼mm. needles and C, cast on 44 sts. and work in K1, P1, rib for 18 rows.
Change to 4mm. needles.
Increase row: K2, inc. in next st., *K1, inc. in next st., rep. from * to last 3 sts., K to end. (64 sts.)
Now starting with a P row work in st. st. in C, **at the same time**, inc. 1 st. at each end of every foll. 6th row until there are 94(94: 94: 100: 100: 100) sts. on the needle.
Now work straight in st. st. until sleeve measures 48(48: 48: 51: 51: 51)cm. (19(19: 19: 20: 20: 20)in.) from cast-on edge, ending with a WS row.
Cast off all sts. fairly loosely.

Neckband

Join right shoulder seam.
With 3¼mm. needles and C and RS facing, pick up and K21 sts. down left front neck, K16 sts. from stitch holder, pick up and K21 sts. up right front neck, K4 sts. down right back neck, K30 sts. from stitch holder and finally pick up and K4 sts. up left back neck. (96 sts.)
Work in K1, P1, rib for 12 rows.
Cast off fairly loosely ribwise.

TO MAKE UP

Press according to ball band instructions.
Join left shoulder and neckband seam. Fold neckband in half to inside and slip stitch loosely in position. Measure and mark 23(23: 23: 24: 24: 24)cm. 9(9: 9: 9½: 9½: 9½)in. each side of shoulder seam and sew sleeves between these marks.
Sew beads or buttons in place for eyes as in picture. With a running stitch embroider fishing line with brown yarn. With a chain stitch and grey embroider fin of fish. Sew button onto box and fish buttons onto stream. Join side and sleeve seams.

44 42 40 38 36 34   34 36 38 40 42 44

131
126
121
116
111
106
101
96
91
86
81
76
71
66
61
56
51
46
41
36
31
26
21
16
11
6
1

Cat and Mouse

MATERIALS

3(3: 4) 25g balls of DOUBLE KNIT-
TING yarn in 1st colour, black (A).
2 balls in 2nd colour, grey (B).
4 balls in 3rd colour, red (C).
1 ball in 4th colour, yellow (D).
1 pair each of 3¼mm. (No. 10) and
4mm. (No. 8) knitting needles.
Small amount of wadding for mouse.
1 black bead for eye.
1 plastic squeaker (optional).
6(6: 7) buttons.
2 stitch holders.
2 safety pins.
*The quantities of yarn given are based
on average requirements and are
therefore approximate.*

MEASUREMENTS

To fit chest 56(61: 66)cm. (22(24:
26)in.)
Actual measurement: 62(67: 73)cm.
(24½(26¾: 29)in.)
Length from shoulder: 38(40: 43)cm.
(15(16: 17)in.)
Sleeve length 28(33: 38)cm. (11(13:
15)in.)
Figures in brackets refer to the larger
sizes. Where only one figure is given
this refers to all sizes.

TENSION

22 sts. and 28 rows to 10cm. (4in.) on
4mm. needles over st. st.

ABBREVIATIONS

K = knit; **P** = purl; **st.(s.)** = stitch(es); **st.
st.** = stocking stitch; **patt.** = pattern;
foll. = following; **inc.** = increase; **dec.**
= decrease; **cont.** = continue; **RS** =
right side; **WS** = wrong side; **rep.** =
repeat; **rem.** = remaining; **A,B,C,D** =
contrast colours; **sl.** = slip; **tog.** = together;
psso. = pass slipped st. over; **mm.** =
millimetres; **cm.** = centimetres; **in.**
= inches.
Note
The lines round the cat's legs and ear,
worked in A, and those bordering the
holes in the cheese, worked in B, may
be embroidered or swiss-darned
when work is complete rather than
knitted, if preferred.

The cat is chasing the mouse, and the mouse is after the
cheese (the pocket) in this marvellously amusing
cardigan modelled by the one and only Francesca O'Brien,
Linda's daughter, who is seven and a half – just the age
Linda was when she started knitting.

INSTRUCTIONS

Back

With 3¼mm. needles and A, cast on 54(60:66)sts. and work in K1, P1, rib for 18 rows.

Change to 4mm. needles.

Increase row: K4(7: 10), inc. in next st., *K3, inc. in next st., rep. from * to last 5(8: 11)sts., K to end of row. (66(72: 78)sts.)

Next row: P.

Place chart

Starting with the 1st row work from **Chart 1**, working between appropriate lines for size required.

Cont. as set until the 42 rows of chart have been worked, thus ending with a WS row.

Now cont. in stripe patt. in st. st. as follows:

Work 4 rows in C, 2 rows in A, 4 rows in C, 2 rows in B.

These 12 rows form the stripe patt. and are repeated to end of garment.

Cont. in stripes as set until back measures 37(39: 42)cm. (14½(15½: 16½)in.) from cast-on edge, ending with a WS row.

Shape back neck

Next row: Patt. 22(25: 28)sts., turn and cont. on this first set of sts. only, placing rem. sts. on a stitch holder.

** Keeping stripes correct, dec. 1 st. at neck edge on next 3 rows.

Cast off rem. 19(22: 25) sts. fairly loosely.

Return to rem. sts. and slip first 22 sts. onto stitch holder. With RS facing rejoin yarn to rem. sts. and patt. to end of row.

Now work as for first side from ** to end.

Left Front

With 3¼mm. needles and A, cast on 27(30:33)sts. and work in K1, P1, rib for 18 rows.

Change to 4mm. needles.

Increase row: K4(7: 10), inc. in next st., *K3, inc. in next st., rep. from * to last 2 sts., K to end of row. (33(36: 39)sts.)

Next row: P. ***

Place chart

Starting with the 1st row work from **Chart 2**, working between appropriate lines for size required.

Cont. as set until the 30 rows of chart have been worked, thus ending with a WS row.

Now cont. in stripe sequence as for back, and cont. straight until front measures 32(34: 37)cm. (12½(13½: 14½)in.) from cast-on edge, ending with a WS row.

Shape front neck

Next row: Patt. 27(30: 33)sts., place last 6 sts. onto a safety pin, turn and keeping stripes correct, dec. 1 st. at neck edge on every row until 19(22: 25)sts. remain.

Now cont. straight in st. st. until front measures the same as back to cast-off shoulder edge, ending with a WS row. Cast off all sts. fairly loosely.

Pocket Lining

With 4mm. needles and D, cast on 25 sts. and starting with a K row work straight in st. st. for 24 rows, thus ending with a WS row.

Leave sts. on a stitch holder.

Right Front

Work as for left front to *** but reverse increase row.

Place chart

Now starting with the 1st row work from **Chart 3**, working between appropriate lines for size required.

Cont. as set until 24 rows of chart have been worked, thus ending with a WS row.

Place pocket

Next row: (25th row of chart) Patt. 5, place next 25 sts. onto stitch holder, then with RS facing, patt. across the 25 sts. from pocket lining, patt. 3(6: 9).

Next row: P across all sts.

Now starting with a K row cont. to follow chart until the 42 rows have been worked, thus ending with a WS row.

Now work as for left front keeping stripe sequence correct, but reversing neck shaping.

Pocket Welt

With 3¼mm. needles and D and RS facing, pick up the 25 sts. from stitch holder and work in K1, P1, rib for 6 rows. Cast off fairly loosely ribwise.

Sleeves

With 3¼mm. needles and A, cast on 36 sts. and work in K1, P1, rib for 18 rows. Change to 4mm. needles.

Increase row: *K1, inc. in next st., rep. from * to end. (54 sts.)

Next row: P.

Now starting with a K row and C, work in st. st and stripe sequence as for back, **at the same time**, inc. 1 st. at each end of 5th and every foll. 6th row until there are 66(72: 78)sts. on the needle, working inc. sts. into stripe patt.

Now work straight in st. st. until sleeve measures 28(33: 38)cm. (11(13: 15)in.) from cast-on edge, ending with a WS row.

Cast off all sts. fairly loosely.

Button Band

With 3¼mm. needles and A and RS facing, pick up and K58(63: 68)sts. evenly along left front (right front for boy) and work in K1, P1, rib for 8 rows. Cast off fairly loosely ribwise.

Buttonhole Band

Work as for button band for 3 rows.

Next row: (Buttonhole row: RS facing) Rib 3, cast off 2 sts., * rib 8(9: 8), cast off 2 sts., rep. from * to last 3 sts., rib to end.

Next row: Rib, casting on 2 sts. over those cast off on previous row. (6(6: 7) buttonholes worked in all.)

Work 3 more rows in rib.

Cast off fairly loosely ribwise.

Collar

Join both shoulder seams.

With 3¼mm. needles and A and RS facing, pick up and K7 sts. from end of buttonhole/button band, K across the 6 sts. from safety pin, pick up and K17 sts. up right front neck, K4 sts. down right back neck, K22 sts. from stitch holder, pick up and K4 sts. up left back neck, K16 sts. down left front neck, K across the 6 sts. from safety pin, and finally pick up and K7 sts. from button/ buttonhole band. (89 sts.)

Next row: (WS facing) P1, *K1, P1, rep. from * to end.

Next row: K1, *P1, K1, rep. from * to end.

Rep. the last 2 rows for 10cm. (4 in.). Cast off all sts. fairly loosely ribwise.

TO MAKE UP

Press according to ball band instructions. Measure and mark 17(18: 19)cm. (6½(7: 7½)in.) each side of shoulder seam and sew sleeves between these marks. Sew pocket lining neatly in position on wrong side and catch stitch pocket welt neatly at sides. With A embroider whiskers on cat, and sew on button for eye. Join side and sleeve seams. Sew on buttons to correspond with buttonholes.

MOUSE

With 3¼mm. needles and B, cast on 33 sts. and starting with a K row work straight in st. st. for 16 rows, thus ending with a WS row.

Shape body

Next row: *K9, K2 tog., rep. from * 3 times. (30 sts.)
Next row: P.
Next row: *K2 tog., K6, K2 tog., rep. from * 3 times. (24 sts.)
Next row: P.

Next row: *K2 tog., K4, K2 tog., rep. from * 3 times. (18 sts.)
Next row: P.
Next row: *K2 tog., K2, K2 tog., rep. from * 3 times. (12 sts.)
Next row: P.
Next row: *K2 tog., rep. from * 6 times. (6 sts.)
Next row: P.
Next row: K3 tog. twice and fasten off.

Ears

With 3¼mm. needles and B, cast on 5 sts. and knit for 4 rows.
5th row: Sl. 1, K1, psso., K1, K2 tog.
6th row: P3 tog. and fasten off.

TO MAKE UP

Seam body of mouse, then thread yarn along cast-on edge, but before pulling up insert squeaker (optional) and stuff with wadding.
Sew ears in place. Embroider face on mouse, add whiskers and make a plait for tail.

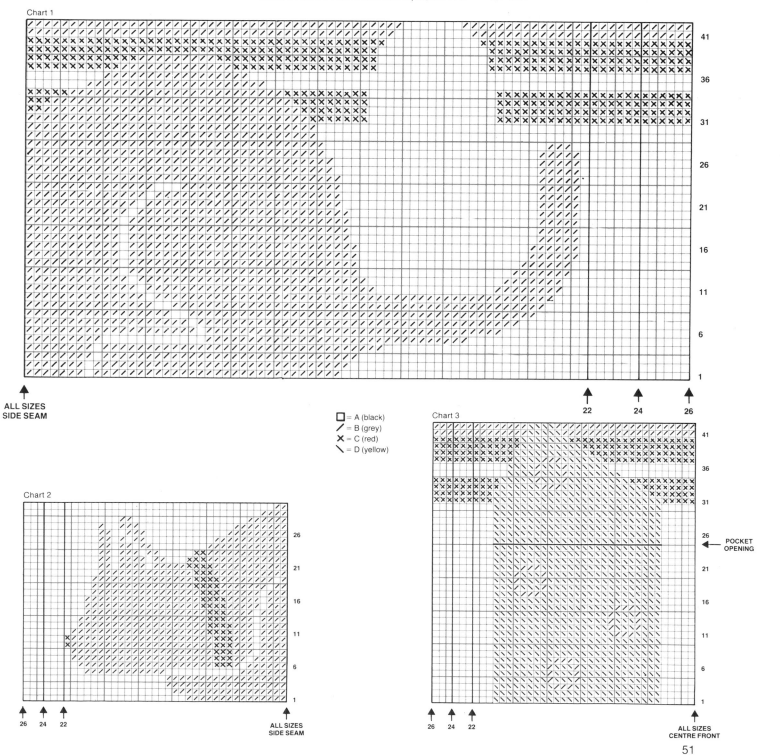

Chart 1

ALL SIZES
SIDE SEAM

□ = A (black)
╱ = B (grey)
✗ = C (red)
╲ = D (yellow)

Chart 2

Chart 3

POCKET OPENING

ALL SIZES
SIDE SEAM

ALL SIZES
CENTRE FRONT

Rib Tickling

MATERIALS

5(5: 6: 6) 50g balls of PATONS DIPLOMA DK in black, main colour (A). 2(2: 2: 3) balls in cream, contrast colour (B).
1 pair each of 3¼mm. (No. 10) and 4mm. (No. 8) knitting needles.
2 stitch holders.
The quantities of yarn given are based on average requirements and are therefore approximate.

MEASUREMENTS

To fit chest: 56(61: 66: 71)cm. (22(24: 26: 28)in.)
Actual measurement: 60(66: 71: 76)cm. (24(26: 28: 30)in.)
Length from shoulder: 38(42: 46: 50)cm. (15(16½: 18: 19¾)in.)
Sleeve length: 28(33: 38: 43)cm. (11(13: 15: 17)in.)
Figures in brackets refer to the larger sizes. Where only one figure is given this refers to all sizes.

TENSION

22 sts. and 30 rows to 10cm. (4in.) on 4mm. needles over st. st.

ABBREVIATIONS

K = knit; **P** = purl; **st.(s.)** = stitch(es); **st. st.** = stocking stitch; **patt.** = pattern; **foll.** = following; **inc.** = increase; **dec.** = decrease; **cont.** = continue; **RS** = right side; **WS** = wrong side; **rep.** = repeat; **rem.** = remaining; **DK** = double knitting; **A** = main colour; **B** = contrast colour; **mm.** = millimetres; **cm.** = centimetres; **in.** = inches.

INSTRUCTIONS

Front
With 3¼mm. needles and A, cast on 54(60: 66: 72)sts. and work in K1, P1, rib for 16 rows.
Change to 4mm. needles.
Increase row: K4(7: 10: 13), inc. in next st., *K3, inc. in next st., rep. from * to last 5(8: 11: 14)sts., K to end of row. (66(72: 78: 84)sts.)
Next row: P.
Place chart
Now starting with the 1st row, work in

T his is my twelve-year-old son Benet Xan Brandreth, doing his best to make a spooktacular impression in this seen-through-X-ray-eyes fun knit. At Hallowe'en it's a must for all. The rest of the year it's the ideal jumper for little horrors (and their ghoul-friends).

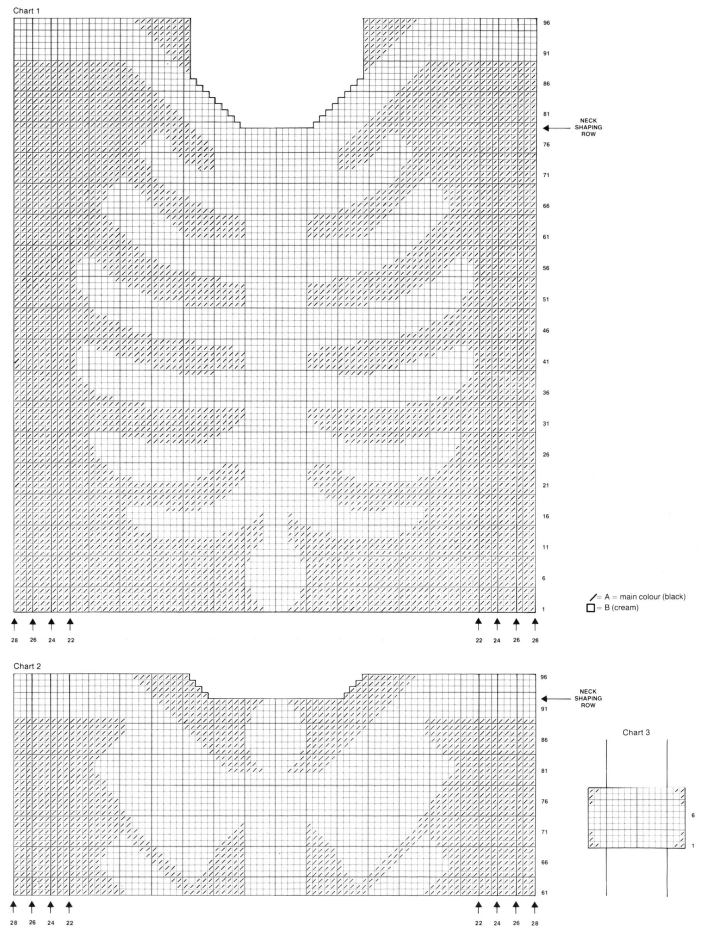

Chart 1

NECK
SHAPING
ROW

/ = A = main colour (black)
□ = B (cream)

96
91
86
81
76
71
66
61
56
51
46
41
36
31
26
21
16
11
6
1

28 26 24 22   22 24 26 28

Chart 2

NECK
SHAPING
ROW

96
91
86
81
76
71
66
61

28 26 24 22   22 24 26 28

Chart 3

6
1

53

st. st. from **Chart 1**, working between appropriate lines for size required. Work the first 12 rows, then rep. them 0(1: 2: 3) time(s) more. (12(24: 36: 48) patt. rows worked.)**

Now starting with the 13th row, work from chart as set until the 78th row of chart has been completed, thus ending with a WS row.

Shape front neck
Next row: (79th row of chart) Patt. 27(30: 33: 36)sts., turn and cont. on this first set of sts. only, placing rem. sts. on a stitch holder. *** Keeping chart correct, dec. 1 st. at neck edge on every row until 19(22: 25: 28)sts. remain.

Now cont. straight until chart is complete (96th row worked).
Cast off all sts. fairly loosely.
Return to rem. sts. and slip first 12 sts. onto stitch holder. With RS facing rejoin yarn to rem. sts. and patt. to end of row.
Now work as for first side from *** to end.

Back
Work as for front to **
Now starting with the 13th row, work from chart as set until the 60th row of chart has been completed, thus ending with a WS row.
Now starting with the 61st row, work from **Chart 2**, working between appropriate lines for size required, as for front.
Cont. as set until 92nd row of chart has been worked, thus ending with a WS row.

Shape back neck
Next row: (93rd row of chart) Patt. 22(25: 28: 31)sts., turn and cont. on this first set of sts. only, placing rem. sts. on a stitch holder.
**** Keeping chart correct, dec. 1 st. at neck edge on next 3 rows (96th row of chart complete).
Cast off rem. 19(22: 25: 28)sts. fairly loosely.
Return to rem. sts. and slip first 22 sts. onto stitch holder. With RS facing rejoin yarn to rem. sts. and patt. to end of row.
Now work as for first side from **** to end.

Sleeves
With 3¼mm. needles and A, cast on 36 sts. and work in K1, P1, rib for 16 rows. Change to 4mm. needles.
Increase row: K2, inc. in next st., *K1, inc. in next st., rep from * to last 3 sts., K to end. (52 sts.)
Next row: P.

Place chart
1st row: (RS facing) K21A, 10B, 21A. Cont. in st. st. and patt. as now set, keeping the centre 10 sts. in A straight, **at the same time**, inc. 1 st. at each end of 5th row and then every foll. 6th row until there are 60(62: 66: 68)sts. on the needle ending with a WS row and working inc. sts. into A at either side. Still keeping inc. as before, work the 10 rows from **Chart 3** as shown, then cont. in the 10-stitch patt. as before and inc. as before until there are 66(72: 78: 84) sts. on the needle.
Now work straight in st. st. and in patt. until sleeve measures 28(33: 38: 43)cm. (11(13: 15: 17)in.) from cast-on edge, ending with a WS row.
Cast off all sts. fairly loosely.

Neckband
Join right shoulder seam matching patt.
With 3¼mm. needles and A and RS facing, pick up and K16 sts. down left front neck, K12 sts. from stitch holder, pick up and K16 sts. up right front neck, K4 sts. down right back neck, K22 sts. from stitch holder and finally pick up and K4 sts. up left back neck. (74 sts.)
Work in K1, P1, rib for 12 rows.
Cast off fairly loosely ribwise.

TO MAKE UP

Press according to ball band instructions.
Join left shoulder and neckband seam. Fold neckband in half to inside and slip stitch loosely in position. Measure and mark 17(18: 19: 20)cm. (6½(7: 7½: 8)in.) each side of shoulder seam and sew sleeves between these marks.
Join side and sleeve seams.

Keeping Warm

MATERIALS

4(4: 4: 5: 5: 5) 50g balls of SIRDAR NOCTURNE MOHAIR in 1st colour, white (A).
5(5: 5: 6: 6: 6) balls in 2nd colour, turquoise (B).
1 ball in each of 3 other colours, rust (C), black (D), and yellow (E).
1 pair each of 4½mm. (No. 7) and 5½mm. (No. 5) knitting needles.
2 small black buttons or beads for eyes.
2 stitch holders.
The quantities of yarn given are based on average requirements and are therefore approximate.

MEASUREMENTS

To fit bust/chest: 86(91: 96: 101: 107: 112)cm. (34(36: 38: 40: 42: 44)in.)
Actual measurement: 93(98: 103: 108: 113: 118)cm. (37(39: 41: 43: 45: 47)in.)
Length from shoulder: 63(65: 68: 70: 70: 70)cm. (25¼(26: 27¼: 28: 28: 28)in.)
Sleeve length: 48(48: 48: 50: 50: 50)cm. (19¼(19¼: 19¼: 20: 20: 20)in.)
Figures in brackets refer to the larger sizes. Where only one figure is given this refers to all sizes.

TENSION

16 sts. and 20 rows to 10cm. (4in.) on 5½mm. needles over st. st.

ABBREVIATIONS

K = knit; **P** = purl; **st.(s.)** = stitch(es); **st. st.** = stocking stitch; **foll.** = following; **inc.** = increase; **dec.** = decrease; **cont.** = continue; **RS** = right side; **WS** = wrong side; **rep.** = repeat; **rem.** = remaining; **patt.** = pattern; **A,B,C,D,E** = contrast colours; **mm.** = millimetres; **cm.** = centimetres; **in.** = inches.
Note
When working bobbles use separate lengths of yarn for each bobble worked.
To make bobbles (RS facing)
K to stitch marked, then with A, K into front and back of next st. twice, and K into front again (5 sts.). Turn, and work 4 rows in st. st., then with left-hand

*P*ick up a penguin? Yes, please, when it's being worn by my friend Su Pollard, one of the funniest, loveliest, most talented people around.

INSTRUCTIONS

Back

With 4½mm. needles and A, cast on 58(62: 66: 70: 74: 78)sts. and work in K1, P1, rib for 16 rows.
Change to 5½mm. needles.
Increase row: K6(8: 10: 4: 6: 8), inc. in next st., *K2(2: 2: 3: 3: 3), inc. in next st., rep from * to last 6(8: 10: 5: 7: 9)sts., K to end of row. (74(78: 82: 86: 90: 94)sts.)
Next row: P. **
Now starting with a K row work straight in st. st. in A for 46(50: 56: 60: 60: 60)

needle take 2nd, 3rd, 4th and 5th sts. over 1st st.

rows, thus ending with a WS row.
Place chart
Change to B and starting with the 1st row work in st.st. from **Chart 1**, working between appropriate lines for size required and working bobbles as indicated. Cont. as set until 58th row of chart has been worked, thus ending with a WS row.
Shape back neck
Next row: (59th row of chart) Patt. 27(29: 31: 33: 35: 37)sts., turn and cont. on this first set of sts. only, placing rem. sts. on a stitch holder.
*** Dec. 1 st. at neck edge on next 3 rows.
Cast off rem. 24(26: 28: 30: 32: 34)sts. fairly loosely.

Chart 1

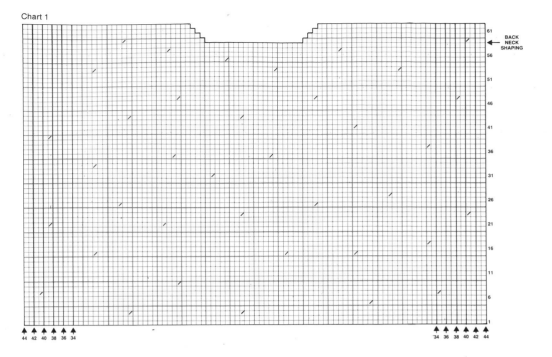

BACK
NECK
SHAPING

44 42 40 38 36 34   '34 36 38 40 42 44

Chart 3

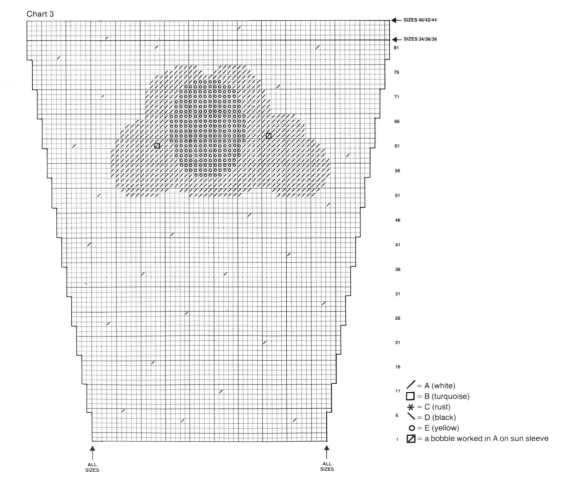

SIZES 40/42/44
SIZES 34/36/38

ALL SIZES   ALL SIZES

/ = A (white)
□ = B (turquoise)
✳ = C (rust)
\ = D (black)
○ = E (yellow)
☑ = a bobble worked in A on sun sleeve

56

Return to rem. sts. and slip first 20 sts. onto stitch holder. With RS facing rejoin yarn to rem. sts. and patt. to end of row.

Now work as for first side from *** to end, keeping chart correct.

Front

Work as for back to **

Now starting with a K row work 0(4: 10: 14: 14: 14) rows straight in st. st. in A, thus ending with a WS row.

Place chart

Now starting with the 1st row work in st. st. from **Chart 2**, working between appropriate lines for size required, and working bobbles as indicated.

Cont. as set until 92nd row of chart has been worked, thus ending with a WS row.

Shape front neck

Next row: (93rd row of chart) Patt. 30(32: 34: 36: 38: 40)sts. turn and cont. on this first set of sts. only, placing rem. sts. on a stitch holder.

*** Keeping bobbles correct, dec. 1 st. at neck edge on every row until 24(26: 28: 30: 32: 34) sts. remain.

Now cont. straight in st. st. following chart until front measures the same as back to shoulder cast-off edge, ending with a WS row.

Cast off all sts. fairly loosely.

Return to rem. sts. and slip first 14 sts. onto stitch holder, with RS facing rejoin yarn to rem. sts. and patt. to end of row.

Now work as for first side from *** to end.

Cloud Sleeve

With 4½mm. needles and B, cast on 32 sts. and work in K1, P1, rib for 14 rows. Change to 5½mm. needles.

Increase row: *K1, inc. in next st., rep. from * to end. (48 sts.)

Next row: P.

Now starting with the 1st row work in st. st. from **Chart 3**, **at the same time** inc. 1 st. at each end of every foll. 6th row, working bobbles as indicated and working only the cloud (omit the sun outline).

Cont. to inc. as set until there are 74 sts. on the needle.

Now work a few rows straight until sleeve measures 48(48: 48: 50: 50: 50)cm. (19¼(19¼: 19¼: 20: 20: 20)in.) from cast-on edge, ending with 82nd(82nd: 82nd: 86th: 86th: 86th) row of chart.

Cast off all sts. fairly loosely.

Sun Sleeve

Work as for cloud sleeve, working bobbles as indicated and working only the sun (omit the cloud outline).

Neckband

Join right shoulder seam.
With 4½mm. needles and B and RS facing, pick up and K14 sts. down left front neck, K14 sts. from stitch holder, pick up and K14 sts. up right front neck, K4 sts. down right back neck, K20 sts. from stitch holder and finally pick up and K4 sts. up left back neck. (70 sts.)
Work in K1, P1, rib for 10 rows.
Cast off fairly loosely ribwise.

TO MAKE UP

Press according to ball band instructions.
Join left shoulder and neckband seam. Fold neckband in half to inside and slip stitch loosely in position. Measure and mark 25cm (10in.) each side of shoulder seam and sew sleeves between these marks.
Sew on beads or buttons for eyes. Using a chain stitch, embroider sun's rays with E as in picture. Join side and sleeve seams.

```
/ = A (white)
□ = B (turquoise)
✳ = C (rust)
\ = D (black)
O = E (yellow)
◨ = a bobble worked in A on sun sleeve
```

Chart 2

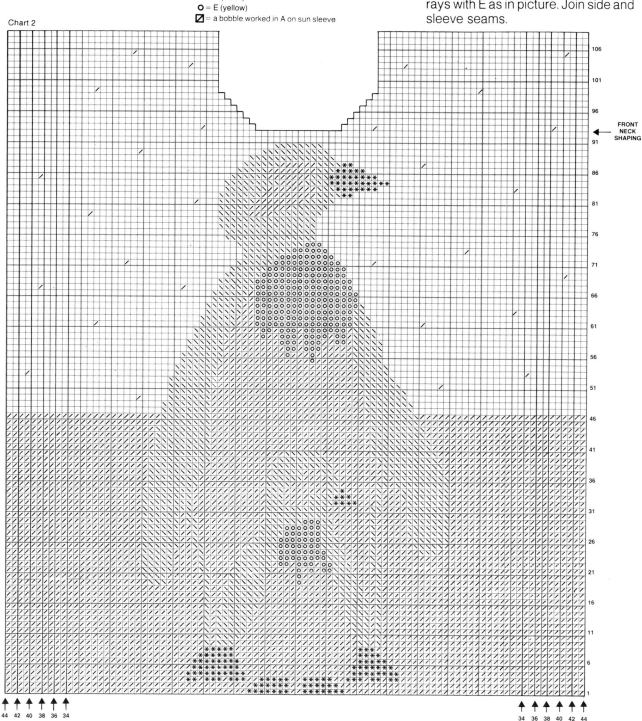

FRONT
NECK
SHAPING

44 42 40 38 36 34

34 36 38 40 42 44

Plain Sailing

MATERIALS

7(7: 8: 8: 9: 9) 50g balls of PATONS DIPLOMA DK in light blue, main colour (C).
2(2: 2: 2: 3: 3) balls in royal blue, 1st contrast (A).
1(1: 2: 2: 2: 2) balls in mid-blue, 2nd contrast (B).
1 ball in each of 5 other contrasting colours, yellow (D), black (E), white (F), green (G) and red (H).
1 pair each of 3¼mm. (No 10) and 4mm. (No 8) knitting needles.
2 stitch holders.
The quantities of yarn given are based on average requirements and are therefore approximate.

MEASUREMENTS

To fit bust / chest: 86(91: 96: 101: 107: 112)cm. (34(36: 38: 40: 42: 44)in.)
Actual measurement: 93(98: 104: 107: 113: 118)cm. (37(39: 41½: 43: 45: 47)in.)
Length from shoulder: 64(67: 70: 72: 72: 72)cm. (25(26: 27: 28: 28: 28)in.)
Sleeve length: 48(48: 48: 51: 51: 51)cm. (19(19: 19: 20: 20: 20)in.)
Figures in brackets refer to the larger sizes. Where only one figure is given this refers to all sizes.

TENSION

22 sts. and 30 rows to 10cm. (4in.) on 4mm. needles over st. st.

ABBREVIATIONS

K = knit; **P** = purl; **st.(s.)** = stitch(es); **st. st.** = stocking stitch; **patt.** = pattern; **foll.** = following; **inc.** = increase; **dec.** = decrease; **cont.** = continue; **RS** = right side; **WS** = wrong side; **rep.** = repeat; **rem.** = remaining; **DK** = double knitting; **C** = main colour; **A,B,D,E,F,G,H** = contrast colours; **mm.** = millimetres; **cm.** = centimetres; **in.** = inches.

ven if you don't know starboard from port (or even from brandy), you'll be riding on the crest of a sartorial wave the moment you don this jolly boating jumper modelled here by the real man in Linda O'Brien's life, her maddeningly handsome and delightful husband Peter.

INSTRUCTIONS

Back

With 3¼mm. needles and A, cast on 84(90: 96: 100: 106: 112)sts. and work in K1, P1, rib for 20 rows.

Change to 4mm. needles.

Increase row: K8(11: 14: 7: 10: 13), inc. in next st., *K3(3: 3: 4: 4: 4), inc. in next st., rep. from * to last 7(10: 13: 7: 10: 13)sts., K to end. (102(108: 114: 118: 124: 130)sts.)

Next row: P.

Now work in sea pattern as follows:

1st row: (RS facing) K2(0: 2: 0: 1: 0)A, 1(0: 1: 0: 1: 0)B, 2(2: 2: 1: 2: 1)A, *3A, 1B, 2A, rep. from * to last 1(4: 1: 3: 0: 3)st.(s.), 1(3: 1: 3: 0: 3)A, 0(1: 0: 0: 0: 0)B.

2nd row: P0(2: 0: 1: 0: 1)B, 1(2: 1: 2: 0: 2)A, *1A, 3B, 2A, rep. from * to last 5(2: 5: 1: 4: 1)st.(s.), 1(1: 1: 1: 1: 1)A, 3(1: 3: 0: 3: 0)B, 1(0: 1: 0: 0: 0)A.

3rd row: K5(2: 5: 1: 4: 1)B, *1A, 5B, rep. from * to last 1(4: 1: 3: 0: 3) st.(s.), 1(1: 1: 1: 0: 1)A, 0(3: 0: 2: 0: 2)B.

4th row: P in B.

Starting with a K row work 4 rows in st. st. in B.

Now rep. these 8 rows once more but reversing colours, i.e. read B for A and A for B.

These 16 rows form the sea patt.**

Cont. in patt. as set until 56 rows in all have been worked, thus ending with a WS row.

Now work first 3 patt. rows again, but using B and C.

Now cont. straight in C only until back measures (62(65: 68: 70: 70: 70)cm. (24½(25½: 26½: 27½: 27½: 27½)in.) from cast-on edge, ending with a WS row.

Shape back neck

Next row: K35(38: 41: 43: 46: 49)sts., turn and cont. on this first set of sts. only, placing rem. sts. on a stitch holder.

*** Dec. 1 st. at neck edge on next 3 rows.

Cast off rem. 32(35: 38: 40: 43: 46) sts fairly loosely.

Return to rem. sts. and slip first 32 sts. onto stitch holder, with RS facing rejoin yarn to rem. sts. and K to end of row. Now work as for first side from *** to end.

Front

Work as for back to **

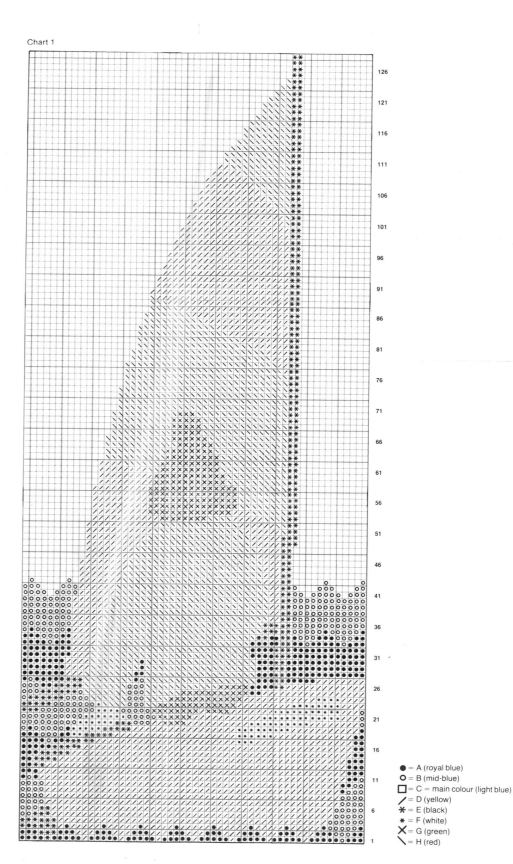

Chart 1

● = A (royal blue)
○ = B (mid-blue)
□ = C = main colour (light blue)
╱ = D (yellow)
✳ = E (black)
✱ = F (white)
✕ = G (green)
╲ = H (red)

Place chart

Now work from **Chart 1** as follows, working sea patt. on either side as set: *1st row:* (RS facing) patt. 23(26: 29: 31: 34: 37), patt. across the 56 sts. of 1st row of chart, patt. 23(26: 29: 31: 34: 37). Cont. as now set until the 128 rows of chart have been worked, then cont. in C until front measures 56(59: 62: 64: 64: 64)cm. (22(23: 24: 25: 25: 25)in.) from cast-on edge, ending with a WS row.

Shape front neck

Next row: K42(45: 48: 50: 53: 56)sts., turn and cont. on this first set of sts. only, placing rem. sts. on a stitch holder.

**** Dec. 1 st. at neck edge on every row until 32(35: 38: 40: 43: 46) sts. remain.

Now cont. straight in st. st. until front measures the same as back to cast-off shoulder edge, ending with a WS row.

Cast off all sts. fairly loosely.

Return to rem. sts. and slip first 18 sts. onto stitch holder. With RS facing rejoin yarn to rem. sts. and K to end of row.

Now work as for first side from **** to end.

Cloud Sleeve

With 3¼mm. needles and C, cast on 44 sts. and work in K1, P1, rib for 20 rows.

Change to 4mm. needles.

Increase row: K2, inc. in next st., *K1, inc. in next st., rep. from * to last 3 sts., K to end. (64 sts.)

Now starting with a P row cont. in st. st.,

inc. 1 st. at each end of every foll. 6th row until there are 88 sts. on the needle, ending with a WS row.

Now place **Chart 2** as follows:

Next row: K16 C, now work across the 56 sts. of 1st row of cloud chart, K16 C. The cloud chart is now set. Cont. to follow chart until complete, **at the same time** inc. as before until there are 94(94: 94: 100: 100: 100)sts. on the needle. Now cont. straight in st. st. and when chart is complete cont. in C only until sleeve measures 48(48: 48: 51: 51: 51)cm. (19(19: 19: 20: 20: 20)in.) from cast-on edge, ending with a WS row.

Cast off all sts. fairly loosely.

Sun Sleeve

Work as for cloud sleeve until there are 90 sts. on the needle, ending with a WS row.

Now place **Chart 3** as follows:

Next row: K35C, now work across the 20 sts. of 1st row of sun chart, K35C. The sun chart is now set. Cont. to follow chart until complete, **at the same time** complete as for cloud sleeve.

Neckband

Join right shoulder seam.

With 3¼mm. needles and C and RS facing, pick up and K20 sts. down left front neck, K18 sts. from stitch holder, pick up and K20 sts. up right front neck, K4 sts. down right back neck, K32 sts. from stitch holder, and finally pick up and K4 sts. up left back neck. (98 sts.) Work in K1, P1, rib for 12 rows.

Cast off fairly loosely ribwise.

Press according to ball band instructions.

Join left shoulder and neckband seam. Turn neckband in half to inside and slip stitch loosely in position. Measure and mark 23(23: 23: 24: 24: 24)cm. (9(9: 9: 9½: 9½: 9½)in.) each side of shoulder seam and sew sleeves between these marks. Using a chain stitch embroider sun's rays with D. With E embroider birds and number on sail as in picture. Any name can be added to the side of the boat. Join side and sleeve seams.

● = A (royal blue)
○ = B (mid-blue)
□ = C = main colour (light blue)
╱ = D (yellow)
✳ = E (black)
✱ = F (white)
✕ = G (green)
╲ = H (red)

Chart 2

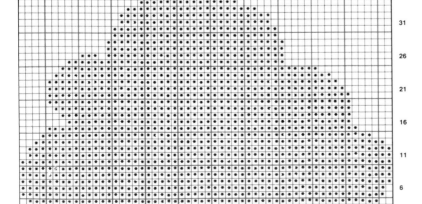

Chart 3

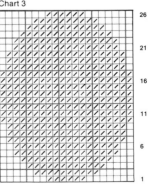

Cat on a Mat

H ere's a purr-fect jumper for a young lady with a purr-
fect figure, my friend Lizzie Webb. *I* say she looks so
good because she was born that way. *She* says it's because
she exercises every day. I've exercised with her on
breakfast television week in week out for four whole years
and what I want to know is why does it work so well for
her and – well, er – not quite so well for me?

MATERIALS

2 50g balls of HAYFIELD GRAMPIAN DK 1st colour, light green (A).
5(5: 5: 6: 6: 6) balls in 2nd colour, pink (B).
1 ball in each of 4 other colours, light brown (C), dark brown (D), mauve (E) and cream (F).
1 pair each of 3¼mm. (No. 10) and 4mm. (No. 8) knitting needles.
2 small black oval buttons or beads for eyes.
2 stitch holders.
The quantities of yarn given are based on average requirements and are therefore approximate.

MEASUREMENTS

To fit chest/bust: 86(91: 96: 101: 107: 112)cm. (34(36: 38: 40: 42: 44)in.)
Actual measurement: 91(96: 102:106: 111: 116)cm. (36(38½: 41: 42: 44: 46½)in.)
Length from shoulder: 63(66: 69: 71: 71: 71)cm. (25(26: 27: 28: 28: 28)in.)
Sleeve length: 48(48: 48: 51: 51: 51)cm. (19(19: 19: 20: 20: 20)in.) Figures in brackets refer to the larger sizes. Where only one figure is given this refers to all sizes.

TENSION

22 sts. and 28 rows to 10cm. (4in.) on 4mm. needles over st. st.

ABBREVIATIONS

K = knit; **P** = purl; **st.(s.)** = stitch(es); **st. st.** = stocking stitch; **foll.** = following; **inc.** = increase; **dec.** = decrease; **cont.** = continue; **RS** = right side; **WS** = wrong side; **rep.** = repeat; **DK** = double knitting; **rem.** = remaining; **A,B,C,D,E,F** = contrast colours; **mm.** = millimetres; **cm.** = centimetres; **in.** = inches.

Note

The outlines round the cat's legs, chin and mouth, worked in C, may be embroidered or swiss-darned when work is complete rather than knitted, if preferred.

INSTRUCTIONS

Back

With 3¼mm. needles and A, cast on 82(88: 94: 98: 104: 110) sts. and work in K1, P1, rib for 18 rows.
Change to 4mm. needles.
Increase row: K6(9: 12: 14: 17: 20), inc. in next st., *K3, inc. in next st., rep. from * to last 7(10: 13: 15: 18: 21)sts., K to end of row. (100(106: 112: 116: 122: 128)sts.)
Next row: P. **
Now starting with a K row work straight in st. st. in A for 46(50: 54: 58: 58: 58) rows, thus ending with a WS row.
Change to B and cont. straight in st. st. until back measures 62(65: 68: 70: 70: 70)cm. (24½(25½: 26½: 27½: 27½: 27½)in.) from cast-on edge, ending with a WS row.

Shape back neck

Next row: K35(38: 41: 43: 46: 49)sts., turn and cont. on this first set of sts. only, placing rem. sts. on a stitch holder.
*** Dec. 1 st. at neck edge on next 3 rows.
Cast off rem. 32(35: 38: 40: 43: 46)sts. fairly loosely.
Return to rem. sts. and slip first 30 sts. onto stitch holder. With RS facing rejoin yarn to rem. sts. and K to end of row.
Now work as for first side from *** to end.

Front

Work as for back to **
Now starting with a K row work straight in st. st. in A for 0(4: 8: 12: 12: 12) rows, thus ending with a WS row.

Place chart

Now starting with the 1st row, work in st. st. from chart, working between appropriate lines for size required.
Cont. as set until the 136 rows of chart have been worked.
Now work a few rows in st. st. in colours as set until front measures 56(59: 62: 64: 64: 64)cm. (22(23: 24: 25: 25: 25)in.) from cast-on edge, ending with a WS row.

Shape front neck

Next row: K42(45: 48: 50: 53: 56)sts; turn and cont. on this first set of sts. only, placing rem. sts. on a stitch holder.
**** Keeping colours as set, dec. 1 st. at neck edge on every row until 32(35: 38: 40: 43: 46)sts. remain.
Now cont. straight in st. st. in colours as set until front measures the same as back to shoulder cast-off edge ending with a WS row.
Cast off all sts. fairly loosely.
Return to rem. sts. and slip first 16 sts. onto stitch holder. With RS facing rejoin yarn to rem. sts. and K to end of row.
Now work as for first side from **** to end.

Sleeves

With 3¼mm. needles and B cast on 44 sts. and work in K1, P1, rib for 18 rows.
Change to 4mm. needles.
Increase row: K2, inc. in next st., *K1, inc. in next st., rep. from * to last 3 sts., K to end. (64 sts.)
Now starting with a P row cont. in st. st. in B, **at the same time**, inc. 1 st. at each end of every foll. 6th row until there are 94(94: 94: 100: 100: 100)sts. on the needle.
Now cont. straight in st. st. until sleeve measures 48(48: 48: 51: 51: 51)cm. (19(19: 19: 20: 20: 20)in.) from cast-on edge, ending with a WS row.
Cast off all sts. fairly loosely.

Neckband

Join right shoulder seam.
With 3¼mm. needles and E and RS facing, pick up and K21 sts. down left front neck, K16 sts. from stitch holder, pick up and K21 sts. up right front neck, K4 sts. down right back neck, K30 sts. from stitch holder and finally pick up and K4 sts. up left back neck. (96 sts.)
Work in K1, P1, rib for 12 rows.
Cast off fairly loosely ribwise.

TO MAKE UP

Press according to ball band instructions.
Join left shoulder and neckband seam. Fold neckband in half to inside and slip stitch loosely in position. Measure and mark 23(23: 23: 24: 24: 24)cm. (9(9: 9: 9½: 9½: 9½)in.) each side of shoulder seam and sew sleeves between marks. Sew beads or buttons in place for eyes. Using a daisy stitch and F, embroider flowers on front, back and sleeves as in picture. Join side and sleeve seams.

Flying a Kite

TENSION

24 sts. and 30 rows to 10cm. (4in.) on 4mm. needles over st. st.

ABBREVIATIONS

K = knit; **P** = purl; **st.(s.)** = stitch(es); **st. st.** = stocking stitch; **foll.** = following; **inc.** = increase; **dec.** = decrease; **cont.** = continue; **RS** = right side; **WS** = wrong side; **rep.** = repeat; **rem.** = remaining; **A** = main colour; **B,C,D** = contrast colours; **DK** = double knitting; **mm.** = millimetres; **cm.** = centimetres; **in.** = inches.

INSTRUCTIONS

Back

With 3¼mm. needles and A, cast on 60(66:72)sts. and work in K1, P1, rib for 16 rows.

Change to 4mm. needles.

Increase row: K2(5: 8), inc. in next st., *K4, inc. in next st., rep. from * to last 2(5: 8)sts., K to end of row. (72(78: 84)sts.)

Next row: P. **

Now starting with a K row work straight in st. st. in A until back measures 24(28: 32)cm. (9½(11: 12½)in.) from cast-on edge, ending with a WS row.

Place chart

Next row: K29(32: 35)A, now work across the 40 sts. of 1st row of **Chart 1**, K3(6: 9)A.

The chart is now placed. Cont. as set until the 24 rows of chart have been worked.

Now cont. straight in A only until back measures 37(40: 42)cm. (14½(15½: 16½)in.) from cast-on edge, ending with a WS row.

Shape back neck

Next row: K25(28: 31)sts., turn and cont. on this first set of sts. only, placing rem. sts. on a stitch holder.

*** Dec. 1 st. at neck edge on next 3 rows.

Cast off rem. 22(25: 28)sts. fairly loosely.

Return to rem. sts. and slip first 22 sts. onto stitch holder. With RS facing rejoin yarn to rem. sts. and K to end of row.

Now work as for first side from *** to end.

Lizzie Webb has a handsome and brilliant son called Ben and here he is modelling our kite sweater. Ben couldn't resist the light-up bow tie to match – as if he needed to prove he was bright as well as a high flyer!

MATERIALS

4(4: 5) 50g balls of SIRDAR COUNTRY STYLE DK in main colour, blue (A).
1 ball in each of 3 other colours, white (B), red (C) and yellow (D). Small amount of black yarn.
1 pair each of 3¼mm. (No. 10) and 4mm. (No. 8) knitting needles.
2 stitch holders.
The quantities of yarn given are based on average requirements and are therefore approximate.

MEASUREMENTS

To fit chest: 56(61: 66)cm. (22(24: 26)in.)
Actual measurement: 60(65: 70)cm. (24(26: 28)in.)
Length from shoulder: 38(41: 43)cm. (15(16: 17)in.)
Sleeve length: 28(33: 38)cm. (11(13: 15)in.)
Figures in brackets refer to the larger sizes. Where only one figure is given this refers to all sizes.

Front

Work as for back to **

Now starting with a K row work straight in st. st. in A until front measures 17(19: 21)cm. (6½(7½: 8½)in.) from cast-on edge, ending with a WS row.

Place chart

Next row: K6(9: 12)A, now work across the 20sts. of 1st row of **Chart 2**, K46(49: 52)A.

Cont. as set until 12 rows of chart have been worked, thus ending with a WS row.

Place chart

Next row: K6(9: 12)A, work across the 13th row of **Chart 2**, K3(6: 9)A, now work across the 40sts. of 1st row of **Chart 1**, K3A.

Cont. as now set until both charts are complete.

Now work straight in A only until front measures 32(35: 37)cm. (12½(13½: 14½)in.) from cast-on edge, ending with a WS row.

Shape front neck

Next row: K30(33: 36)sts., turn and cont. on this first set of sts. only, placing rem. sts. on a stitch holder.

**** Dec. 1 st. at neck edge on every row until 22(25: 28)sts. remain.

Now cont. straight until front measures the same as back to shoulder cast-off edge, ending with a WS row.

Cast off all sts. fairly loosely.

Return to rem. sts. and slip first 12 sts. onto stitch holder. With RS facing rejoin yarn to rem. sts. and K to end of row.

Now work as for first side from **** to end.

Sun Sleeve

With 3¼mm. needles and A, cast on 38 sts. and work in K1, P1, rib for 14 rows. Change to 4mm. needles.

Increase row: *K1, inc. in next st., rep. from * to last 2 sts., K2. (56 sts.)

Now starting with a P row cont. in st. st. in A, **at the same time**, inc. 1 st. at each end of every foll. 6th row until there are 68(72: 76)sts. on the needle, ending with a WS row. //

Place chart

Next row: K26(28: 30)A, now work across the 16 sts. of 1st row of **Chart 3**, K26(28: 30)A.

Cont. as set and complete the 20 rows of chart, **at the same time** keeping incs. as before on every foll. 6th row until there are 72(78: 84)sts. on the

needle.

Now cont. straight in A until sleeve measures 28(33: 38)cm. (11(13: 15)in.) from cast-on edge, ending with a WS row.

Cast off all sts. fairly loosely.

Cloud Sleeve

Work as for sun sleeve to //.

Place chart

Next row: K14(16: 18)A, now work across the 40 sts. of 1st row of **Chart 1**. K14(16: 18)A.

Cont. as set and complete the 24 rows of chart, and complete as for sun sleeve.

Bows

(Make 4 of each in C and D)

With 3¼mm. needles and appropriate colour, cast on 6 sts. and knit for 12 rows. Cast off.

Neckband

Join right shoulder seam.

With 3¼mm. needles and A and RS facing, pick up and K17 sts. down left front neck, K12 sts. from stitch holder, pick up and K17 sts. up right front neck, K4 sts. down right back neck, K22 sts. from stitch holder and finally pick up and K4 sts. up left back neck. (76 sts.)

Work in K1, P1, rib for 12 rows.

Cast off fairly loosely ribwise.

TO MAKE UP

Press according to ball band instructions.

Join left shoulder and neckband seam. Fold neckband in half to inside and slip stitch loosely in position. Measure and mark 17(18: 19)cm. 6½(7: 7½)in. each side of shoulder seam and sew sleeves between these marks. Using a running stitch and black yarn embroider string of kite as in picture. Using a chain stitch embroider sun's rays with D. Wind yarn tightly around centre of bows to give a knot effect, then sew in place as in picture. Join side and sleeve seams.

Chart 1
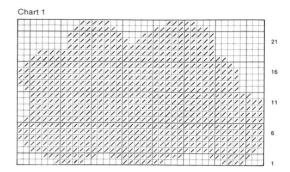

Chart 2
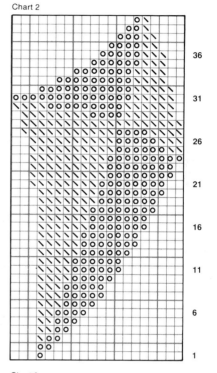

Chart 3
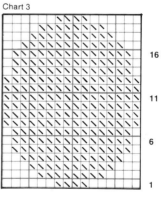

☐ = A = main colour (blue)
╱ = B (white)
○ = C (red)
╲ = D (yellow)

Come Rain, Come Shine

MATERIALS

2 25g balls of DOUBLE KNITTING yarn in 1st colour, charcoal grey (A). 3(3: 4) balls in each of 2 other colours, blue (B) and silver grey (C). 1 ball in each of 3 other colours, yellow (D), white (E) and peach (F). Small amount of black yarn. 1 pair each of 3¼mm. (No. 10) and 4mm. (No. 8) knitting needles. 4 small black beads or buttons. 6(6: 7) buttons. 2 safety pins. 3 stitch holders. *The quantities of yarn given are based on average requirements and are therefore approximate*

MEASUREMENTS

To fit chest: 56(61: 66)cm. (22(24: 26)in.)
Actual measurement: 62(67: 73)cm. (24¾(26¾: 28¾)in.)
Length from shoulder: 38(40: 43)cm. (15(16: 17)in.)
Sleeve length: 28(33: 38)cm. (11(13: 15)in.)
Figures in brackets refer to the larger sizes. Where only one figure is given this refers to all sizes.

TENSION

22 sts. and 28 rows to 10cm. (4in.) on 4mm. needles over st. st.

ABBREVIATIONS

K = knit; **P** = purl; **st.(s.)** = stitch(es); **st. st.** = stocking stitch; **patt.** = pattern; **foll.** = following; **inc.** = increase; **dec.** = decrease; **cont.** = continue; **RS** = right side; **WS** = wrong side; **rep.** = repeat; **rem.** = remaining; **A,B,C,D,E,F** = contrast colours; **mm.** = millimetres; **cm.** = centimetres; **in.** = inches.

INSTRUCTIONS

Back

With 3¼mm. needles and A, cast on 54(60:66)sts. and work in K1, P1, rib for 18 rows.
Change to 4mm. needles.
Increase row: K4(7: 10), inc. in next st., *K3, inc. in next st., rep. from * to last

The rain it raineth every day
 Upon the just and unjust fella
But more upon the just
 Because the unjust hath the just's umbrella!
The moral of the verse is that in this life you may sometimes get wet – but if you wear this delightful cardigan you'll always be warm. It's being modelled by George Lewis, a seven-year-old famous for his sunny disposition.

5(8: 11)sts., K to end of row. (66(72: 78)sts.)
Next row: P.
Now work in two colour pattern as follows:
Next row: (RS facing) K33(36: 39)B, K33(36: 39)C.
Cont. in st. st. in this way working the two halves in different colours until back measures 20(23: 25)cm. (8(9: 10)in.) from cast-on edge, ending with a WS row.

Place chart
1st row: K33(36: 39)B, K9(10: 11)C, now work across the 14 sts. of 1st row of **Chart 1**, K10(12: 14)C.
The chart is now set. Cont. to follow chart until the 22 rows have been worked, thus ending with a WS row.

Place charts
1st row: K2(4: 6)B, now work across the 30 sts. from 1st row of **Chart 2** using E for cloud, K1(2: 3)B, K1(2: 3)C, work across the 30 sts. from 1st row of **Chart 2** using A for cloud, K2(4: 6)C.
The charts are now set. Cont. to follow charts until the 20 rows have been worked, thus ending with a WS row.
Now work straight in st. st. using B and C as before until back measures 37(39: 42)cm. (14½(15½: 16½)in.) from cast-on edge, ending with a WS row.

Shape back neck
Next row: K22(25: 28)sts., turn and cont. on this first set of sts. only, placing rem. sts. on a stitch holder.
** Dec. 1 st. at neck edge on next 3 rows.
Cast off rem. 19(22: 25) sts. fairly loosely.
Return to rem. sts. and slip first 22 sts. onto stitch holder. With RS facing rejoin yarn to rem. sts. and K to end of row.
Now work as for first side from ** to end.

Pocket Lining (make 1 in B and 1 in C)
With 4mm. needles and either B or C, cast on 25 sts. and starting with a K row work straight in st. st. for 26 rows, thus ending with a WS row.
Leave sts. on a stitch holder.

Left Front
With 3¼mm. needles and A, cast on 27(30: 33)sts. and work in K1, P1, rib for 18 rows.
Change to 4mm. needles.

Increase row: K4(7: 10), inc. in next st., *K3, inc. in next st., rep. from * to last 2 sts., K to end of row. (33(36: 39)sts.)
Next row: P.
Now work as follows using C as the background colour throughout.

Place chart
1st row: K6(9: 12)C, now work across the 19 sts. of 1st row of **Chart 3**, K8C.
The chart is now set. Cont. to follow chart until the 22 rows have been worked, thus ending with a WS row.
Now cont. in st. st. in C for 4 rows.

Place pocket
Next row: (RS facing) K3(6: 9)C, place next 25 sts. onto stitch holder, and then with RS facing, K across the 25 sts. from first (C) pocket lining, K5C.
Next row: P across all sts.
Now starting with a K row work 4(10: 16) rows in st. st., thus ending with a WS row.

Place chart
1st row: K10(12: 14)C, now work across the 14 sts. from 1st row of **Chart 1**, K9(10: 11)C.
The chart is now set. Cont. to follow chart until the 22 rows have been worked, thus ending with a WS row.

Place chart
1st row: K2(4: 6)C, now work across the 30 sts. from 1st row of **Chart 2** using A for cloud, K1(2: 3)C.
The chart is now set. Cont. to follow chart until front measures 32(34: 37)cm. (12½(13½: 14½)in.) from cast-on edge, ending with a WS row.

Shape front neck
Keeping chart correct cont. as follows:
Next row: Patt. 27 (30: 33)sts., place last 6 sts. onto a safety pin, turn and dec. 1 st. at neck edge on every row until 19(22: 25)sts. remain.
Now cont. straight in st. st. and when chart is complete cont. in C only until front measures the same as back to cast-off shoulder edge, ending with a WS row.
Cast off all sts. fairly loosely.

Right Front
With 3¼mm. needles and A, cast on 27(30: 33)sts. and work in K1, P1, rib for 18 rows.
Change to 4mm. needles.
Increase row: K2, inc. in next st., *K3, inc. in next st., rep. from * to last 4(7: 10)sts., K to end of row. (33(36: 39)sts.)
Next row: P.
Now work as follows using B as the background colour throughout.

Chart 1
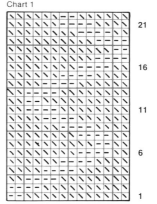

Chart 2
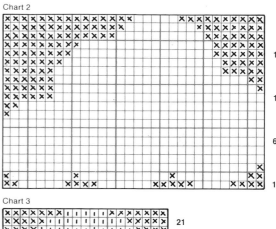

Chart 3
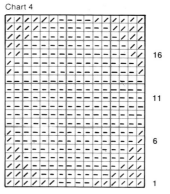

Chart 4
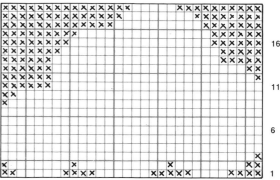

☐ = A (charcoal grey) or E (white) (clouds)
╱ = B (blue)
╲ = C (silver grey)
— = D (yellow)
╵ = F (peach)
✕ = B or C (background to faces)

Place chart

1st row: K8B, now work across the 19 sts. of 1st row of **Chart 3** K6(9: 12)B. The chart is now set. Cont. to follow chart until the 22 rows have been worked, thus ending with a WS row. Now cont. in st. st. in B for 4 rows.

Place pocket

Next row: (RS facing) K5B, place next 25 sts. onto stitch holder, and then with RS facing K across the 25 sts. from second (B) pocket lining, K3(6: 9)B. Now starting with a P row work 27(33: 39) rows in st. st; thus ending with a WS row.

Place chart

1st row: K1(2: 3)B, now work across the 30 sts. from 1st row of **Chart 2** using E for cloud, K2(4: 6)B. The chart is now set. Cont. to follow chart until front measures 32(34: 37)cm. (12½(13½: 14½)in.) from cast-on edge, ending with RS row.

Shape front neck

Keeping chart correct, cont. as follows:

Next row: Patt. 27(30: 33)sts., place last 6 sts. onto a safety pin, turn and dec. 1 st. at neck edge on every row until 19(22: 25)sts. remain. Now cont. straight in st. st. and when chart is complete, cont. in B only until front measures the same as back to cast-off shoulder edge, ending with a WS row.

Cast off all sts. fairly loosely.

Pocket Welt (alike – work 1 in B and 1 in C)

With 3¼mm. needles and either B or C and RS facing, pick up the 25 sts. from stitch holder and work in K1, P1, rib for 6 rows.

Cast off fairly loosely ribwise.

Sun Sleeve

With 3¼mm. needles and B, cast on 36 sts. and work in K1, P1, rib for 18 rows. Change to 4mm. needles.

Increase row: *K1, inc. in next st., rep. from * to end. (54 sts.) ***

Now starting with a P row work in st. st. in B, **at the same time**, inc. 1 st. at each end of every foll. 6th row until there are 64(68: 72)sts. on the needle, ending with a WS row.

Place chart

1st row: K24(26: 28)B, now work across the 16 sts. from 1st row of **Chart 4**, K24(26: 28)B. The chart is now set. Cont. to follow chart until the 20 rows have been worked, **at the same time**, keeping incs. correct as before on every foll. 6th row until there are 66(72: 78)sts. on the needle.

Now work straight in st. st. in B until sleeve measures 28(33: 38)cm. (11(13: 15)in.) from cast-on edge, ending with a WS row.

Cast off all sts. fairly loosely.

Cloud Sleeve

Using C instead of B, work as for sun sleeve to ***

Now starting with a P row work in st. st. in C, **at the same time**, inc. 1 st. at each end of every foll. 6th row until there are 58(62: 66)sts. on the needle, ending with a WS row.

Place chart

1st row: K22(24: 26)C, now work across the 14 sts. from 1st row of **Chart 1**, K22(24: 26)C.

Cont. to inc. as before and complete the 22 rows of chart, thus ending with a WS row. (64(68: 72)sts.)

Place chart

1st row: Inc. in 1st st., K16(18: 20)C, now work across the 30 sts. from 1st row of **Chart 2** using A for cloud, K16(18: 20)C, inc. in last st.

Complete the 20 rows of chart, **at the same time**, inc. as before on the 2 *larger sizes only*, until there are 66(72: 78)sts. on the needle.

Now complete as for sun sleeve using C in place of B.

Button Band

With 3¼mm. needles and A and RS facing, pick up and K58(63: 68)sts.

evenly along left front (right front for boy) and work in K1, P1, rib for 8 rows. Cast off fairly loosely ribwise.

Buttonhole Band

Work as for button band for 3 rows.

Next row: (Buttonhole row: RS facing) Rib 3, cast off 2 sts., *rib 8(9: 8), cast off 2 sts., rep. from * to last 3 sts., rib to end.

Next row: Rib, casting on 2 sts. over those cast off on previous row (6(6: 7) buttonholes worked in all).

Work 3 more rows in rib.

Cast off fairly loosely ribwise.

Collar

Join both shoulder seams.

With 3¼mm. needles and A and RS facing, pick up and K7 sts. from end of buttonhole/button band, K across the 6 sts. from safety pin, pick up and K17 sts. up right front neck, K4 sts. down right back neck, K22 sts. from stitch holder, pick up and K4 sts. up left back neck, K16 sts. down left front neck, K across the 6 sts. from safety pin, and finally pick up and K7 sts. from button/buttonhole band. (89 sts.)

Next row: (WS facing) P1, *K1, P1, rep. from * to end.

Next row: K1, *P1, K1, rep. from * to end.

Rep. the last 2 rows for 10cm. (4 in.). Cast off all sts. fairly loosely ribwise.

TO MAKE UP

Press according to ball band instructions.

Measure and mark 17(18: 19)cm. (6½(7: 7½)in.) each side of shoulder and sew sleeves between these marks. Embroider faces, sun's rays and rain as in picture. Sew on beads for eyes. Sew pocket linings neatly in position on wrong side and catch stitch pocket welts neatly at sides. Join side and sleeve seams. Sew on buttons to correspond with buttonholes.

Stained Glass

MATERIALS

5(5: 5: 5: 5: 6) 50g balls of MOHAIR yarn in 1st colour, black (A).
2(2: 2: 2: 3: 3) balls in each of 3 other colours, mauve (B), lemon (C) and light blue (D).
2 balls in each of 2 other colours, light pink (E) and green (F).
1 ball in each of 2 other colours, purple (G) and fuchsia (H).
1 pair each of 4½mm. (No. 7) and 5½mm. (No. 5) knitting needles.
9 buttons.
3 stitch holders.
2 safety pins
The quantities of yarn given are based on average requirements and are therefore approximate.

MEASUREMENTS

To fit bust: 81(86: 91: 96: 101:)cm. (32(34: 36: 38: 40: 42)in.)
Actual measurement: 93(98:103:108: 113:118)cm. (37(39:41:43:45:47)in.)
Length from shoulder: 76cm. (30in.)
Sleeve length: 51cm. (20in.)
Figures in brackets refer to the larger sizes. Where only one figure is given this refers to all sizes.

TENSION

16 sts. and 20 rows to 10cm. (4in.) on 5½mm. needles over st. st.

ABBREVIATIONS

K = knit; **P** = purl; **st.(s.)** = stitch(es); **st. st.** = stocking stitch; **foll.** = following; **inc.** = increase; **dec.** = decrease; **cont.** = continue; **RS** = right side; **WS** = wrong side; **patt.** = pattern; **rem.** = remaining; **A,B,C,D,E,F,G,H,** = contrast colours; **mm.** – millimetres; **cm.** = centimetres; **in.** = inches.

All the splendour of a medieval cathedral glows in this wonderfully cosy mohair jacket modelled by a fabulous actress, a fine writer and a great beauty called Nanette Newman.

Chart 1

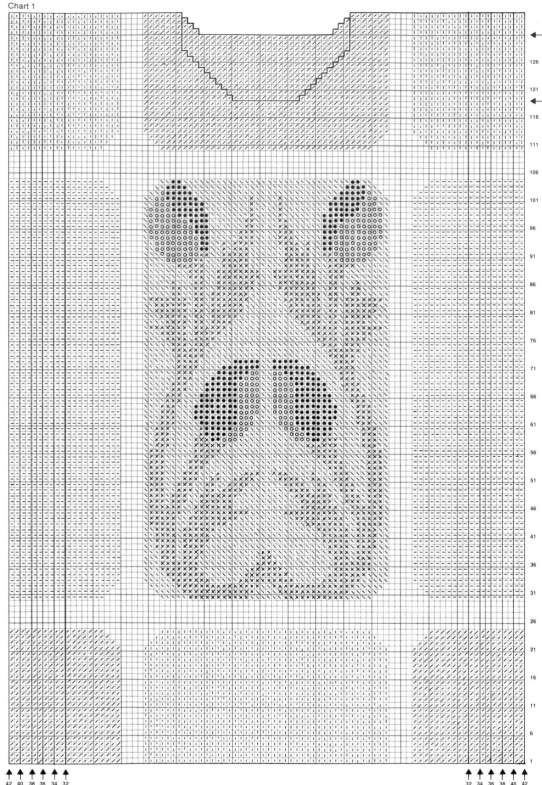

← BACK NECK SHAPING ROW

126
121
116
111
106
101
96
91
86
81
76
71
66
61
56
51
46
41
36
31
26
21
16
11
6
1

42 40 38 36 34 32   32 34 36 38 40 42

□ = A (black)
╱ = B (mauve)
| = C (lemon)
— = D (light blue)
╲ = E (light pink)
✕ = F (green)
● = G (purple)
○ = H (fuchsia)

INSTRUCTIONS

Back
With 4½mm. needles and A, cast on 64(68: 72: 72: 76: 80)sts. and work in K1, P1, rib for 32 rows.
Change to 5½mm. needles.
Increase row: K7(9: 11: 8: 10: 12), inc. in next st., *K6(6: 6: 4: 4: 4), inc. in next st., rep. from * to last 7(9: 11: 8: 10: 12), sts., K. to end of row. (72(76: 80: 84: 88: 92)sts.)
Next row: P.
Now starting with a K row work straight in st. st. from 1st row of **Chart 1**, working between appropriate lines for size required.
Cont. straight as set until 130th row of chart has been worked, thus ending with a WS row.
Shape back neck
Next row: (131st row of chart) Patt. 24(26: 28: 30: 32: 34)sts., turn and cont. on this first set of sts. only, placing rem. sts. on a stitch holder.
** Dec. 1 st. at neck edge on next 3 rows.
Cast off rem 21(23: 25: 27: 29: 31)sts. fairly loosely.
Return to rem. sts. and slip first 24 sts. onto stitch holder. With RS facing rejoin yarn to rem. sts. and patt. to end of row.
Now work as for first side from ** to end, keeping chart correct.

Pocket Lining (make 2)
With 5½mm. needles and C, cast on 25 sts. and starting with a K row work straight in st. st. for 24 rows, thus ending with a WS row.
Leave sts. on a stitch holder.

Left Front
With 4½mm. needles and A, cast on 32(34: 36: 36: 38: 40)sts. and work in K1, P1, rib for 32 rows.
Change to 5½mm. needles.
Increase row: K7(9: 11: 8: 10: 12), inc. in next st., *K6(6: 6: 4: 4: 4) inc. in next st., rep. from * to last 3(3: 3: 2: 2: 2)sts., K to end of row. (36(38: 40: 42: 44: 46)sts.)

Next row: P.

Now starting with a K row work straight in st. st. from 1st row of **Chart 1**, working from appropriate size arrows from side seam to centre front.

Cont. as set until 24 rows of chart have been worked, thus ending with a WS row.

Place pocket

Next row: (25th row of chart) K3(5: 7: 9: 11: 13)A, put next 25 sts. onto a stitch holder and with RS facing patt. across the 25 sts. of one pocket lining, K8A. Now cont. working from chart until 118th row has been worked, thus ending with WS row.

Shape front neck

Next row: (119th row of chart) Patt. 30(32: 34: 36: 38: 40)sts., put last 6 sts. onto a safety pin, turn and dec. 1 st. at neck edge on every row until 21(23: 25: 27: 29: 31)sts. remain.

Now cont. straight following chart until front measures the same as back to shoulder cast-off edge ending with a WS row.

Cast off all sts. fairly loosely.

Pocket Welt

With 4½mm. needles and A and RS facing, pick up the 25 sts. from stitch holder and work in single rib as follows:

1st row: (RS facing) K1, *P1, K1, rep. from * to end.

2nd row: P1, *K1, P1, rep. from * to end. Rep. these 2 rows once more (4 rib rows worked in all).

Cast off fairly loosely ribwise.

Right Front and Pocket Welt

Work as for left front and pocket welt, reversing all shapings and working from appropriate section of chart.

Sleeves

With 4½mm. needles and A, cast on 34 sts. and work in K1, P1, rib for 24 rows.

Change to 5½mm. needles.

Increase row: K4, inc. in every st. to last 4 sts., K to end. (60 sts.)

Next row: P.

Now starting with a K row work in st. st. from 1st row of **Chart 2**, **at the same time**, inc. 1 st. at each end of 5th row and then every foll. 4th row until there are 88 sts. on the needle, working inc. sts. into the chart on either side.

Now cont. straight until chart is complete, thus ending with a WS row.

Cast off all sts. fairly loosely.

Collar

Join both shoulder seams matching patt.

With 4½mm. needles and A and RS facing, K across the 6 sts. from right front safety pin, pick up and K15 sts. to shoulder, K4 sts. down right back, K24 sts. from back stitch holder, pick up and K4 sts. up to shoulder and K15 sts. down the left front, and finally K6 sts. from safety pin (74 sts).

Work in K1, P1, rib for 20cm. (8in.).

Cast off fairly loosely ribwise.

Buttonhole Band

With 4½mm. needles and A, loosely cast on 108 sts. and work in K1, P1, rib for 2 rows.

Next row: (Buttonhole row) *Rib 5 sts., cast off 2 sts., rib 5 sts., rep. from * to end.

Next row: Rib, casting on 2 sts. over those cast-off on previous row. (9 buttonholes worked.)

Rib 4 rows.

Rep. buttonhole rows once more.

Rib 1 row.

Cast off fairly loosely ribwise.

Button Band

Work as for buttonhole band omitting buttonholes.

TO MAKE UP

Press according to ball band instructions.

Measure and mark 29cm. (11½ in.) each side of shoulder seam, and matching patt. Sew sleeves between these marks. Sew pocket linings and welts neatly in position on fronts. Join side and sleeve seams. Turn collar, hem and sleeve ribs in half to inside and slip stitch neatly in position. From top of collar edge to bottom of hem rib, sew front bands to fronts evenly and neatly, then fold in half to inside and slip stitch in position, oversewing buttonholes together.

Sew on buttons to correspond with buttonholes.

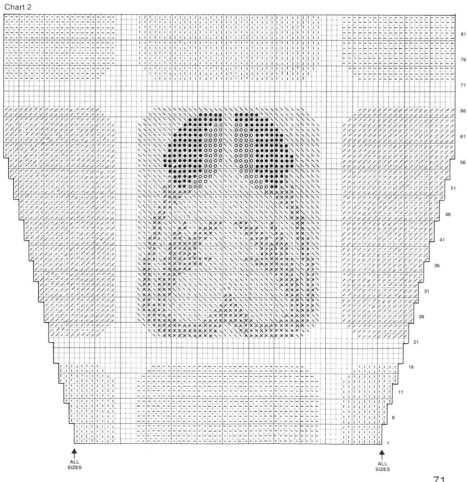

Chart 2

Rabbit Family

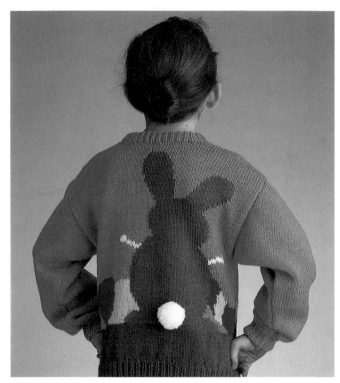

MATERIALS

4 50g balls of HAYFIELD GRAMPIAN DK in light blue, main colour (B).
1 50g ball in each of 5 contrasting colours: green (A), brown (C), yellow (D), red (E) and cream (F).
1 pair each of 3¼mm. (No 10) and 4mm. (No 8) knitting needles.
2 stitch holders.
4 small buttons or beads for eyes.
The quantities of yarn given are based on average requirements and are therefore approximate.

MEASUREMENTS

To fit chest: 56(61: 66)cm. (22(24: 26)in.)
Actual measurement: 60(66: 71)cm. (24(26: 28)in.)
Length from shoulder: 39(41: 44)cm. (15¼(16¼: 17¼)in.)
Sleeve length: 28(33: 38)cm. (11(13: 15)in.)
Figures in brackets refer to the larger sizes. Where only one figure is given this refers to all sizes.

The baby rabbits on the front are being kept warm by a scarf knitted by Mother Rabbit on the back, in this delightful outfit modelled by Aphra Brandreth – who has an appropriate joke to share with you. What do you get if you spill tea down a rabbit warren? A hot, cross bunny!

TENSION

22 sts. and 28 rows to 10cm. (4in.) on 4mm. needles over st. st.

ABBREVIATIONS

K = knit; **P** = purl; **st.(s.)** = stitch(es); **st. st.** = stocking stitch; **foll.** = following; **inc.** = increase; **dec.** = decrease; **cont.** = continue; **RS** = right side; **WS** = wrong side; **rep.** = repeat; **rem.** = remaining; **B** = main colour; **DK** = double knitting; **A,C,D,E,F** = contrast colours; **mm.** = millimetres; **cm.** = centimetres; **in.** = inches.

INSTRUCTIONS

Back

With 3¼mm. needles and A, cast on 54(60:66)sts. and work in K1, P1, rib for 18 rows.

Change to 4mm. needles.
Increase row: K4(7:10), inc. in next st., *K3, inc. in next st., rep. from * to last 5(8: 11)sts., K to end. (66(72: 78)sts.)
Next row: P.
Starting with a K row, work 2(8: 14) rows in st. st.**
Place chart
Now starting with the 1st row, work from **Chart 1**, working between appropriate lines for size required.
Cont. working from chart as set until the 80th row has been worked, then cont. in B only until back measures 37(39: 42)cm. (14½(15½: 16½)in.) from cast-on edge, ending with a WS row.
Shape back neck
Next row: K22(25: 28)sts., turn and cont. on this first set of sts. only, placing rem. sts. on a stitch holder.
*** Dec. 1 st. at neck edge on next 3 rows.

Cast off rem. 19(22: 25)sts. fairly loosely.
Return to rem. sts. and slip first 22 sts. onto stitch holder. With RS facing rejoin yarn to rem. sts. and K to end of row.
Now work as for first side from *** to end.

Front

Work as for back to **

Place chart

Now starting with the 1st row, work from **Chart 2** working between appropriate lines for size required.
Cont. working from chart as set until the 40th row has been worked, then cont. straight in B until front measures 32(34: 37)cm. (12½(13½: 14½)in.) from cast-on edge, ending with a WS row.

Shape front neck

Next row: K27(30: 33)sts., turn and cont. on this first set of sts. only, placing rem. sts. on a stitch holder.
**** Dec. 1st. at neck edge on every row until 19(22: 25)sts. remain.
Now cont. straight until front measures the same as back to cast-off shoulder edge, ending with a WS row.
Cast off all sts. fairly loosely.
Return to rem. sts. and slip first 12 sts. onto stitch holder, with RS facing rejoin yarn to rem. sts. and K to end of row.
Now work as for first side from **** to end.

Sleeves

With 3¼mm. needles and B, cast on 36 sts. and work in K1, P1, rib for 18 rows.
Change to 4mm. needles.
Increase row: *K1, inc. in next st., rep. from * to end. (54 sts.)
Starting with a P row cont. in st. st., inc. 1 st. at each end of every foll. 6th row until there are 66(72: 78)sts. on the needle.
Now cont. straight in st. st. until sleeve measures 28(33: 38)cm. (·11(13: 15)in.) from cast-on edge, ending with a WS row.
Cast off all sts. fairly loosely.

Neckband

Join right shoulder seam.
With 3¼mm. needles and B and RS facing, pick up and K17 sts. down left front neck, K12 sts. from stitch holder, pick up and K17 sts. up right front neck, K4 sts. down right back neck, K22 sts. from stitch holder, and finally pick up and K4 sts. up left back neck. (76 sts.)

Work in K1, P1, rib for 12 rows.
Cast off fairly loosely ribwise.

TO MAKE UP

Press carefully according to ball band instructions.
Join left shoulder and neckband seam. Fold neckband in half to inside and slip stitch loosely in position. Measure and mark 17(18: 19)cm. (6½(7: 7½)in.) each side of shoulder seam and sew sleeves between these marks. Sew beads or buttons in place for eyes. Make a fringe in D for end of scarf.

TO MAKE POMPON

Wind F around two fingers approximately 90 times - cut yarn. With a length of yarn, thread between fingers and tie and knot securely several times tightly around centre of wound yarn. When secure, cut looped ends of yarn. Trim with sharp scissors to shape pompon.

TO COMPLETE

Sew pompon in place on back rabbit as in picture.
Join side and sleeve seams.

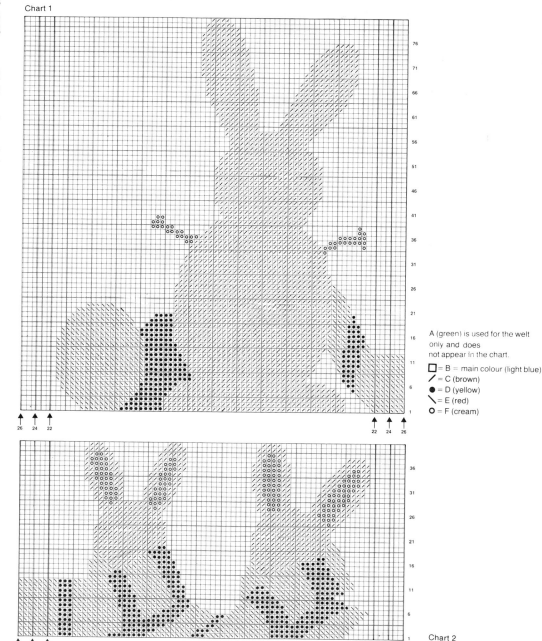

Chart 1

Chart 2

A (green) is used for the welt only and does not appear in the chart.

□ = B = main colour (light blue)
╱ = C (brown)
● = D (yellow)
╲ = E (red)
○ = F (cream)

London Transport

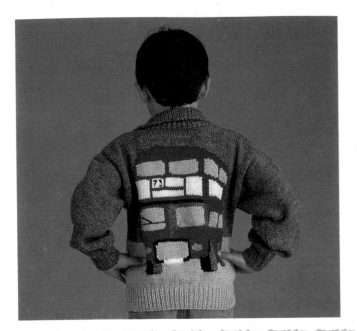

This big six-wheeler, diesel-engined, 97-horse-power omnibus is modelled by George Lewis. It's a veritable transport of delight!

MATERIALS

2(2: 3) 25g balls of DOUBLE KNITTING yarn in 1st colour, silver grey (A).
6(7: 7) balls in 2nd colour, charcoal grey (B).
1 ball in each of 3 other colours, black (C), red (D) and cream (E).
Small amount of yellow (F).
1 pair each of 3¼mm. (No. 10) and 4mm. (No. 8) knitting needles.
6(6: 7) buttons.
3 stitch holders.
2 safety pins.
The quantities of yarn given are based on average requirements and are therefore approximate.

MEASUREMENTS

To fit chest: 56(61: 66)cm. (22(24: 26)in.)
Actual measurement: 62(67: 73)cm. (24¾(26¾: 28¾)in.)
Length from shoulder: 38(40: 43)cm. (15(16: 17)in.)
Sleeve length: 28(33: 38)cm. (11(13: 15)in.)
Figures in brackets refer to the larger sizes. Where only one figure is given this refers to all sizes.

TENSION

22 sts. and 28 rows to 10cm. (4in.) on 4mm. needles over st. st.

ABBREVIATIONS

K = knit; **P** = purl; **st.(s.)** = stitch(es); **st. st.** = stocking stitch; **foll.** = following; **inc.** = increase; **dec.** = decrease; **cont.** = continue; **RS** = right side; **WS** = wrong side; **rep.** = repeat; **rem.** = remaining; **A,B,C,D,E,F** = contrast colours; **mm.** = millimetres; **cm.** = centimetres; **in.** = inches.

INSTRUCTIONS

Back

With 3¼mm. needles and A, cast on 54(60:66)sts. and work in K1, P1, rib for 18 rows.
Change to 4mm. needles.
Increase row: K4(7: 10), inc. in next st., *K3, inc. in next st., rep. from * to last 5(8: 11)sts., K to end of row. (66(72: 78)sts.)
Next row: P.
Now starting with a K row work 0(4: 8) rows in st. st. in A, thus ending with a WS row.

Place chart

1st row: K8(11: 14)A, now work across the 50 sts. of 1st row of chart, K8(11: 14)A.
The chart is now set. Cont. to work in st. st. from chart until 30(26: 22) rows of chart have been worked thus ending with a WS row. Now change background colour from A to B at appropriate size arrow – please note chart is correct for size 56cm. (22in.) only. Cont. as now set until the 80 rows of chart have been worked, thus ending with a WS row.
Now cont. in B only and work straight until back measures 37(39: 42)cm. (14½(15½: 16½)in.) from cast-on edge, ending with a WS row.
Shape back neck
Next row: K22(25: 28)sts., turn and cont. on this first set of sts. only, placing rem. sts. on a stitch holder.
** Dec. 1 st. at neck edge on next 3 rows.
Cast off rem. 19(22: 25)sts. fairly loosely.
Return to rem. sts. and slip first 22 sts. onto stitch holder. With RS facing rejoin yarn to rem. sts. and K to end of row.
Now work as for first side from ** to end.

Pocket Lining (make 2)

With 4mm. needles and A, cast on 25 sts. and starting with a K row work straight in st. st. for 24 rows, thus

74

ending with a WS row.
Leave sts. on a stitch holder.

Left Front

With 3¼mm. needles and A, cast on 27(30:33)sts. and work in K1, P1, rib for 18 rows.
Change to 4mm. needles.
Increase row: K4(7:10), inc. in next st., *K3, inc. in next st., rep. from * to last 2 sts., K to end of row. (33(36:39)sts.)
Next row: P.
Now starting with a K row work straight in st. st. in A for 24 rows, thus ending with a WS row.

Place pocket

Next row: K3(6:9), place next 25 sts. onto stitch holder, and then with RS facing, K across the 25 sts. from first pocket lining, K5.
Next row: P across all sts.
Now starting with a K row work 4 rows in st. st., thus ending with a WS row.
Now change to B and cont. straight in st. st. until front measures 32(34: 37)cm. (12½(13½: 14½)in.) from cast-on edge, ending with a WS row.

Shape front neck
Next row: K27(30:33)sts., place last 6 sts. onto a safety pin, turn and dec. 1 st. at neck edge on every row until 19(22: 25)sts. remain. Now cont. straight in st. st. until front measures the same as back to cast-off shoulder edge, ending with a WS row.
Cast off all sts. fairly loosely.

Right Front

Work as for left front but reverse increase row, pocket placing and neck shaping.

Pocket Welt (alike)

With 3¼mm. needles and A and RS facing, pick up the 25 sts. from stitch holder and work in K1, P1, rib for 6 rows.
Cast off fairly loosely ribwise.

Sleeves

With 3¼mm. needles and B, cast on 36 sts. and work in K1, P1, rib for 18 rows.
Change to 4mm. needles.
Increase row: *K1, inc. in next st., rep. from * to end. (54 sts.)
Now starting with a P row work in st. st. in B, **at the same time,** inc. 1 st. at each end of every foll. 6th row until there are 66(72: 78)sts. on the needle.
Now work straight in st. st. until sleeve measures 28(33: 38)cm. (11(13: 15)in.) from cast-on edge, ending with a WS row.

Cast off all sts. fairly loosely.

Button Band

With 3¼mm. needles and B and RS facing, pick up and K58(63: 68)sts. evenly along left front (right front for boy) and work in K1, P1, rib for 8 rows.
Cast off fairly loosely ribwise.

Buttonhole Band

Work as for button band for 3 rows.
Next row: (Buttonhole row: RS facing) Rib 3, cast off 2 sts., *rib 8(9: 8), cast off 2 sts., rep. from * to last 3 sts., rib to end.
Next row: Rib, casting on 2 sts. over those cast off on previous row (6(6: 7) buttonholes worked in all).
Work 3 more rows in rib.
Cast off fairly loosely ribwise.

Collar

Join both shoulder seams.
With 3¼mm. needles and B and RS facing, pick up and K7 sts. from end of buttonhole/button band, K across the 6 sts. from safety pin, pick up and K17 sts. up right front neck, K4 sts. down right back neck, K22 sts. from stitch holder, pick up and K4 sts. up left back neck, K16 sts. down left front neck, K across the 6 sts. from safety pin, and finally pick up and K7 sts. from button/ buttonhole band. (89 sts.)
Next row: (WS facing) P1, *K1, P1, rep. from * to end.
Next row: K1, *P1, K1, rep. from * to end.
Rep. the last 2 rows for 10cm. (4in.).
Cast off all sts. fairly loosely ribwise.

TO MAKE UP

Press according to ball band instructions.
Measure and mark 17(18: 19)cm. (6½(7: 7½)in.) each side of shoulder seam and sew sleeves between these marks.
With C embroider windscreen wiper and number of bus as in picture. Sew pocket linings neatly in position on wrong side and catch stitch pocket welts neatly at sides. Join side and sleeve seams. Sew on buttons to correspond with buttonholes.

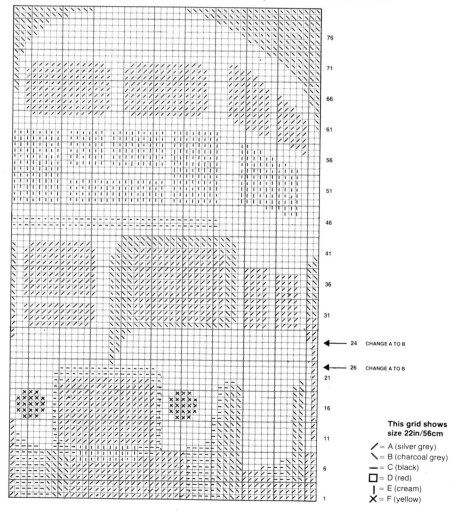

76
71
66
61
56
51
46
41
36
31

← 24 CHANGE A TO B
← 26 CHANGE A TO B

21
16
11
6
1

This grid shows
size 22in/56cm

╱ = A (silver grey)
╲ = B (charcoal grey)
— = C (black)
□ = D (red)
⌐ = E (cream)
✕ = F (yellow)

On the Beach

Anneka Rice has travelled the world – by land, by sea, by air – and she likes to travel light. When she's in sunny seaside resorts she likes nothing better than to wear this incredible cotton sweater in wonderful vibrant colours. It's just the thing to slip over your swimsuit when the sun's gone down.

MATERIALS

4(4: 4: 5: 5: 5) 50g balls of DOUBLE KNITTING COTTON in yellow, 1st colour (A).
1 ball in each of 4 other colours, brown (B), red (C), white (D) and royal blue (E).
3 balls in 6th colour, green (F).
8 balls in 7th colour, light blue (G).
1 pair each of 3¼mm. (No. 10) and 4mm. (No. 8) knitting needles.
2 stitch holders.
The quantities of yarn given are based on average requirements and are therefore approximate.

MEASUREMENTS

To fit bust/chest: 81(86: 91: 96: 101)cm. (32(34: 36: 38: 40: 42)in.)
Actual measurement: 88(92: 96: 102: 106: 110)cm. (35¼(37: 38½: 41: 42½: 44)in.)
Length from shoulder: 66cm. (26in.)
Sleeve length: 50cm. (19½in.).
Figures in brackets refer to the larger sizes. Where only one figure is given this refers to all sizes.

TENSION

20 sts. and 26 rows to 10cm. (4in.) on 4mm. needles over st. st.

ABBREVIATIONS

K = knit; **P** = purl; **st.(s.)** = stitch(es); **st. st.** = stocking stitch; **foll.** = following; **inc.** = increase; **dec.** = decrease; **cont.** = continue; **RS** = right side; **WS** = wrong side; **rep.** = repeat; **rem.** = remaining; **patt.** = pattern; **A,B,C,D,E,F,G** = contrast colours; **mm.** = millimetres; **cm.** = centimetres; **in.** = inches.
Note
The top of the glass, worked in E, the drinking straw, worked in D, and the hatband, worked in C, may be embroidered or swiss-darned when work is complete rather than knitted, if preferred.

INSTRUCTIONS

Front
With 3¼mm. needles and A, cast on 62(66: 70: 72: 76: 80)sts. and work in K1, P1, rib for 18 rows.
Change to 4mm. needles.
Increase row: K5(7: 9: 6: 8: 10), inc. in next st., *K1, inc. in next st., rep. from * to last 6(8: 10: 7: 9: 11)sts., K to end of row. (88(92: 96: 102: 106: 110)sts.)
Next row: P.
Now starting with a K row work straight in st. st. in A for 10 rows, thus ending with a WS row.
Place chart
Now starting with the 1st row, work in st. st. from **Chart 1**, working between appropriate lines for size required. Cont. as set until 132nd row of chart has been worked, thus ending with a WS row.
Shape back neck
Next row: (133rd row of chart) Patt. 32(34: 36: 39: 41: 43)sts.; turn and cont. on this first set of sts. only, placing rem. sts. on a stitch holder.
**Keeping patt. correct, dec. 1 st. at neck edge on every row until 24(26: 28: 31: 33: 35)sts. remain. Work 1 row thus ending with a WS row.
Cast off all sts. fairly loosely.
Return to rem. sts. and slip first 24 sts. onto stitch holder. With RS facing rejoin yarn to rem. sts. and patt. to end of row.
Now work as for first side from ** to end.
Back
Work exactly as for front but when working from **Chart 1** omit deck chair, drink, towel and hat.

Plain Sleeve
With 3¼mm. needles and G, cast on 36 sts. and work in K1, P1, rib for 14 rows.
Change to 4mm. needles.
Increase row: K4, inc. in next 28 sts., K4. (64 sts.)
Now starting with a P row cont. in st. st. in G, **at the same time**, inc. 1 st. at each end of every foll. 4th row until there are 106 sts. on the needle.
Now cont. straight in st. st. until sleeve measures 46cm. (18in.) from cast-on edge, ending with a WS row.
Shape top
Cast off 6 sts. at beginning of next 10 rows.
Cast off rem. 46 sts. fairly loosely.
Sun Sleeve
Work as for plain sleeve, but inc. on every foll. 4th row until there are 92 sts. on the needle, ending with a WS row.

Place chart
Next row: K33G, work across the 26 sts. of 1st row of **Chart 2**, K33G.
The chart is now set. Cont. to work the 34 rows of chart, **at the same time** keeping incs. correct on every foll. 4th row as set until there are 106 sts. on the needle.
Complete to match plain sleeve.

Neckband
Join right shoulder seam.
With 3¼mm. needles and F and RS facing, pick up and K11 sts. down left front neck, K24 sts. from stitch holder, pick up and K11 sts. up right front neck, K11 sts. down right back neck, K24 sts. from stitch holder and finally pick up and K11 sts. up left back neck. (92 sts.)
Starting with a K row work in st. st. for 8 rows.
Cast off fairly loosely.

TO MAKE UP

Press according to ball band instructions.
Join left shoulder and neckband seam. Fold neckband in half to inside and slip stitch loosely in position. Measure and mark 28cm. (11in.) each side of shoulder seam and sew sleeves between these marks. Using A and a chain stitch, work sun's rays as in picture. Join side and sleeve seams.

\ = A (yellow)
/ = G (light blue)

Chart 2

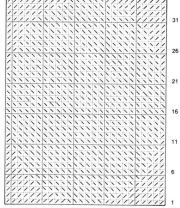

Chart 1

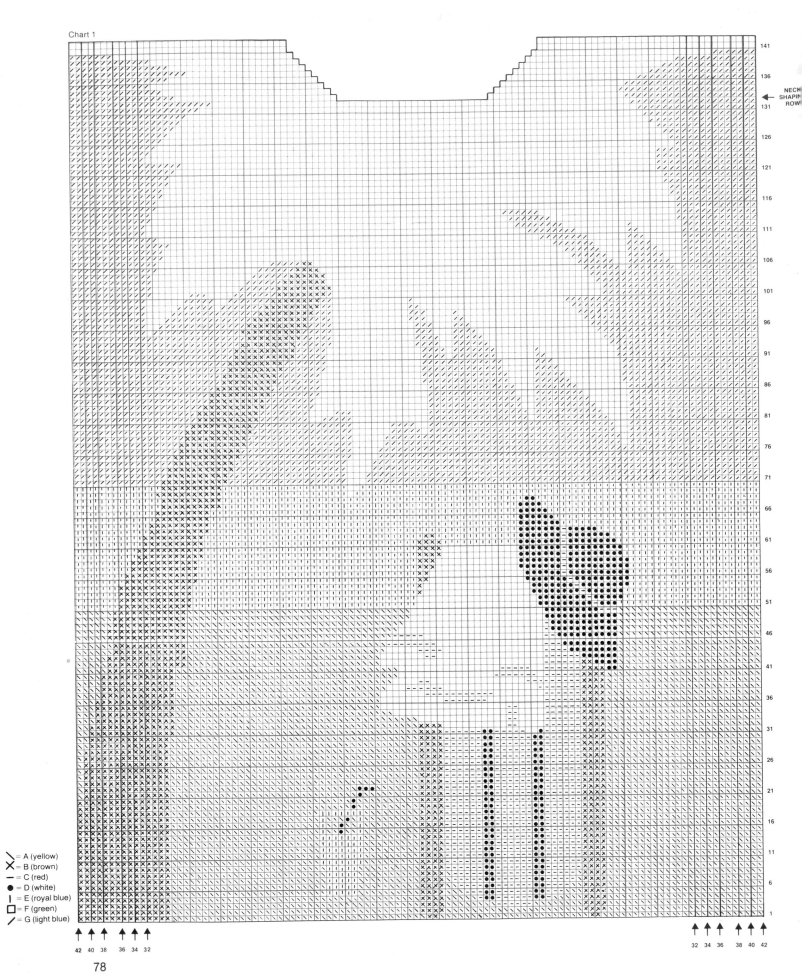

NECK SHAPING ROW

141
136
131
126
121
116
111
106
101
96
91
86
81
76
71
66
61
56
51
46
41
36
31
26
21
16
11
6
1

⟍ = A (yellow)
✕ = B (brown)
— = C (red)
● = D (white)
| = E (royal blue)
□ = F (green)
╱ = G (light blue)

42 40 38   36 34 32   32 34 36   38 40 42

Spellbound

MATERIALS

11(12: 13) 25g balls of DOUBLE KNITTING yarn in main colour, grey (A).
1 ball in each of 4 other colours, white (B), red (C), black (D) and yellow (E)
1 pair each of 3¼mm. (No. 10) and 4mm. (No. 8) knitting needles.
10 yellow star buttons and 3 square black beads or buttons.
2 stitch holders.
1 medium-sized crochet hook.
The quantities of yarn given are based on average requirements and are therefore approximate.

MEASUREMENTS

To fit chest/bust: 71(76: 81)cm. (28(30: 32)in.)
Actual measurement: 75(80: 86)cm. (30(32: 34)in.)
Length from shoulder: 48(53: 58)cm. (19(21: 23)in.)
Sleeve length: 42(44: 47)cm. (16½(17½: 18½)in.)
Figures in brackets refer to the larger sizes. Where only one figure is given this refers to all sizes.

TENSION

22 sts. and 28 rows to 10cm. (4in.). on 4mm. needles over st. st.

ABBREVIATIONS

K = knit; **P** = purl; **st.(s.)** = stitch(es); **st. st.** = stocking stitch; **foll.** = following; **inc.** = increase; **dec.** = decrease; **cont.** = continue; **RS** = right side; **WS** = wrong side; **rep.** = repeat; **rem.** = remaining; **A** = main colour; **B,C,D,E** = contrast colours; **mm.** = millimetres; **cm.** = centimetres; **in.** = inches.
Note
The line showing the rim of the cauldron, worked in D, may be embroidered or swiss-darned when work is complete rather than knitted, if preferred.

INSTRUCTIONS

Back

With 3¼mm. needles and A, cast on 70(76: 82)sts. and work in K1, P1, rib for

S ixteen-year-old Aled Jones is spellbound by this bewitching jumper, which comes in three teenage sizes. (Aled has a special timepiece to go with this outfit: a witch-watch!)

18 rows.
Change to 4mm. needles.
Increase row: K12(15: 18), inc. in next st., *K3, inc. in next st., rep. from * to last 13(16: 19)sts., K to end of row. (82(88: 94)sts.)
Next row: P. **

Now starting with a K row work straight in st. st. in A until back measures 47(52: 57)cm. (18½(20½: 22½)in.) from cast-on edge, ending with a WS row.

Shape back neck
Next row: K28(31: 34)sts., turn and

cont. on this first set of sts. only, placing rem. sts. on a stitch holder.
*** Dec. 1 st. at neck edge on next 3 rows.
Cast off rem 25(28: 31)sts. fairly loosely.
Return to rem. sts. and slip first 26 sts. onto stitch holder. With RS facing rejoin yarn to rem. sts. and K to end of row.
Now work as for first side from *** to end.

Front

Work as for back to **
Now starting with a K row work straight in st. st. in A for 4(18: 32) rows, thus ending with a WS row.

Place chart

1st row: K10(13: 16) A, now work across the 62 sts. from 1st row of chart, K10(13: 16) A.
The chart is now set. Cont. to follow chart until the 90 rows of chart are worked.
Now work straight in A until front measures 42(47: 52)cm. (16½(18½: 20½)in.) from cast-on edge, ending with a WS row.

Shape front neck

Next row: K34(37: 40)sts., turn and cont. on this first set of sts. only, placing rem. sts. on a stitch holder.
**** Dec. 1 st. at neck edge on every row until 25(28: 31)sts. remain.
Now cont. straight in st. st. until front measures the same as back to shoulder cast-off edge, ending with a WS row.
Cast off all sts. fairly loosely.
Return to rem. sts. and slip first 14 sts. onto stitch holder. With RS facing rejoin yarn to rem. sts. and K to end of row.
Now work as for first side from **** to end.

Sleeves

With 3¼mm. needles and A, cast on 40 sts. and work in K1, P1, rib for 18 rows.
Change to 4mm. needles.
Increase row: K6, inc. in next st., *K1, inc. in next st., rep. from * to last 7 sts., K to end. (54 sts.)
Now starting with a P row cont. in st. st in A, **at the same time**, inc. 1 st. at each end of every foll. 6th row until there are 80(84: 88)sts. on the needle.
Now cont. straight in st. st. until sleeve measures 42(44: 47)cm. (16½(17½: 18½)in. from cast-on edge, ending

with a WS row.
Cast off all sts. fairly loosely.

Neckband

Join right shoulder seam.
With 3¼mm. needles and A and RS facing, pick up and K18 sts. down left front neck, K14 sts. from stitch holder, pick up and K18 sts. up right front neck, K4 sts. down right back neck, K26 sts. from stitch holder and finally pick up and K4 sts. up left back neck. (84 sts.)
Work in K1, P1, rib for 12 rows.
Cast off fairly loosely ribwise.

□ = A = main colour (grey)
O = B (white)
╲ = C (red)
╱ = D (black)
✳ = E (yellow)

TO MAKE UP

Press according to ball band instructions.
Join left shoulder and neckband seam. Fold neckband in half to inside and slip stitch loosely in position. Measure and mark 20(21: 22)cm. (7½(8: 8½)in.) each side of shoulder seam and sew sleeves between these marks. Sew on black beads or buttons for witch's and snake's eyes. With D embroider witch's smile, spider's legs and thread, and bat's eyes. With E embroider spider's eyes, then make hair with strands of E looped through with a crochet hook. Sew on stars as in picture. Join side and sleeve seams.

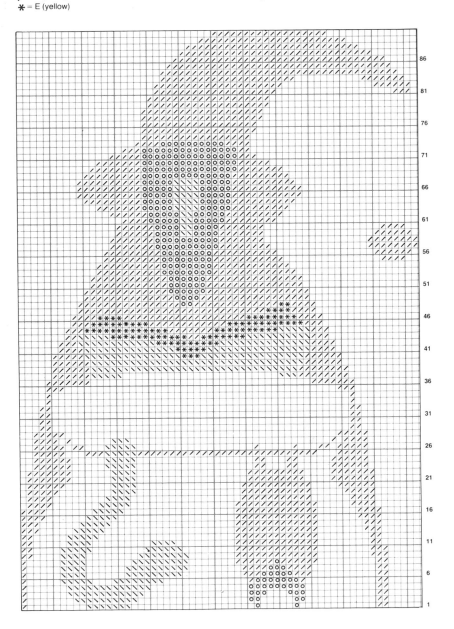

Snake and Ladder

MATERIALS

11(11: 12: 12: 12: 13) 50g balls of LISTER ARAN in navy, main colour (A).
2 balls in each of 2 contrasting colours, green (B) and yellow (C).
Small amount in each of white (D) and red (E).
1 pair each of 4mm. (No. 8) and 5mm. (No. 6) knitting needles.
2 buttons or beads for eyes.
2 stitch holders.
The quantities of yarn given are based on average requirements and are therefore approximate.

MEASUREMENTS

To fit chest/bust: 86(91: 96: 101: 107: 112)cm. (34(36: 38: 40: 42: 44)in.)
Actual measurement: 91(96: 100: 107: 111: 116)cm. (36(38: 40: 42: 44: 46)in.)
Length from shoulder: 63(66: 69: 71: 71: 71)cm. (25(26: 27: 28: 28: 28)in.)
Sleeve length: 48(48: 48: 51: 51: 51)cm. (19(19: 19: 20: 20: 20)in.)
Figures in brackets refer to the larger sizes. Where only one figure is given this refers to all sizes.

TENSION

18 sts. and 22 rows to 10 cm. (4in.) on 5mm. needles over st. st.

ABBREVIATIONS

K = knit; **P** = purl; **st.(s.)** = stitch(es); **st. st.** = stocking stitch; **patt.** = pattern; **foll.** = following; **inc.** = increase; **dec.** = decrease; **cont.** = continue; **RS** = right side; **WS** = wrong side; **rep.** = repeat; **rem.** = remaining; **A** = main colour; **B,C,D,E** = contrasting colours; **mm.** = millimetres; **cm.** = centimetres; **in.** = inches.

INSTRUCTIONS

Back
With 4mm. needles and A, cast on 66(70: 74: 80: 84: 88)sts., and work in K1, P1, rib. for 16 rows.
Change to 5mm. needles.
Increase row: K2(4: 6: 9: 11: 13), inc. in next st., *K3, inc. in next st., rep. from * to last 3(5: 7: 10: 12: 14)sts., K to end

of row. (82(86: 90: 96: 100: 104)sts.)
Next row: P.
Now starting with a K row work straight in st. st. for 2(8: 14: 20: 20: 20) rows.**
Place chart
Now starting with the 1st row, work in

st. st. from **Chart 1**, working between appropriate lines for size required. Cont. as set until the 38 rows of chart are complete.
Now work straight in st. st. in A for a further 48 rows, ending with a WS row.

Here I am, inspired by the temptation of Eve, trying to look wonderfully wicked in this strong and stylish sweater – which probably looks even better on a real man.

Place chart

Now starting with the 1st row work in st. st. from **Chart 2**, working between appropriate lines for size required until 28th row of chart has been completed, thus ending with a WS row.

Shape back neck

Next row: (29th row of chart) Patt. 31(33: 35: 38: 40: 42)sts., turn and cont. on this first set of sts. only, placing rem. sts. on a stitch holder.

*** Keeping chart correct, dec. 1 st. at neck edge on next 3 rows. (32nd row of chart complete.)

Cast off rem 28(30: 32: 35: 37: 39)sts. fairly loosely.

Return to rem. sts. and slip first 20 sts. onto stitch holder. With RS facing rejoin yarn to rem. sts. and patt. to end of row.

Now work as for first side from *** to end.

Front

Work as for back to **

Place chart

Now starting with the 1st row work in st. st. from **Chart 3**, working between appropriate lines for size required. Cont. straight working from chart until 102nd row of chart has been worked, thus ending with a WS row.

Shape front neck

Next row: (103rd row of chart) Patt. 35(37: 39: 42: 44: 46)sts., turn and cont. on this first set of sts. only, placing rem. sts. on a stitch holder.

**** Keeping chart correct, dec. 1 st. at neck edge on every row until 28(30: 32: 35: 37: 39)sts. remain.

Now cont. straight until chart is complete (118th row worked).

Cast off all sts. fairly loosely. (Front measures same as back.)

Return to rem. sts. and slip first 12 sts. onto stitch holder. With RS facing rejoin yarn to rem. sts. and patt. to end of row.

Now work as for first side from **** to end.

Sleeves

With 4mm. needles and A, cast on 36 sts. and work in K1, P1, rib for 14 rows. Change to 5mm. needles.

Increase row: *K1, inc. in next 2 sts., rep. from * to end. (60 sts.)

Now starting with a P row cont. in st. st. and A, inc. 1 st. at each end of every foll. 6th row until there are 80(80: 80: 88: 88: 88)sts. on the needle.

Now cont. straight in st. st. until sleeve measures 48(48: 48: 51: 51: 51)cm. (19(19: 19: 20: 20: 20)in.) from cast-on edge, ending with a WS row.

Cast off all sts. fairly loosely.

Neckband

Join right shoulder seam matching patt.

With 4mm. needles and A and RS facing, pick up and K17 sts. down left front neck, K12 sts. from stitch holder, pick up and K17 sts. up right front neck, K4 sts. down right back neck, K20 sts. from stitch holder and finally pick up

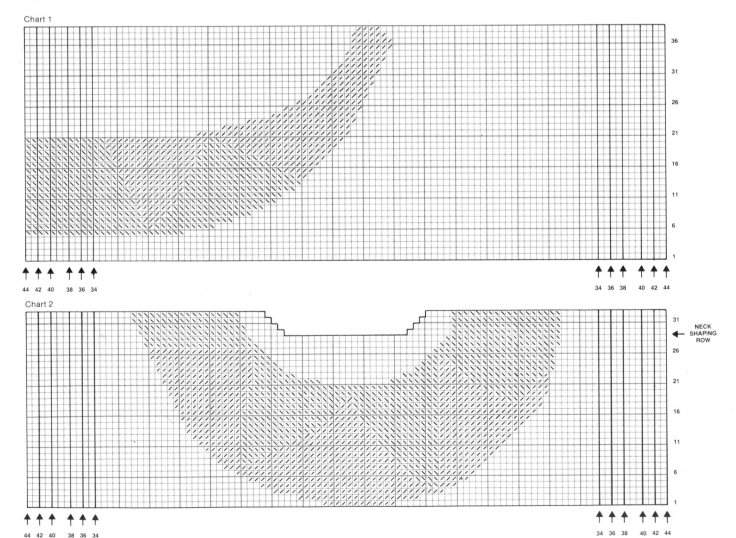

82

and K4 sts. up left back neck. (74 sts.)
Work in K1, P1, rib for 10 rows.
Cast off fairly loosely ribwise.

TO MAKE UP

Press according to ball band
instructions.
Join left shoulder and neckband seam
matching patt. Fold neckband in half to
inside and slip stitch loosely in position. Measure and mark 24(24: 24: 27:
27: 27)cm. 9½(9½: 9½: 10½: 10½:
10½)in. each side of shoulder seams
and sew sleeves between these
marks. Sew beads or buttons in place
for eyes.

To make tongue: With E and 12
strands of yarn, tightly plait for 3cm.
(1¼in.), then cont. plait in 2 bunches of
6 strands. When these are also 3cm.
(1¼in.) secure both ends with a knot.
Sew tongue in place.
Join side and sleeve seams matching
patt.

☐ = A = main colour (navy)
╱ = B (green)
╲ = C (yellow)
✳ = D (white)

Chart 3

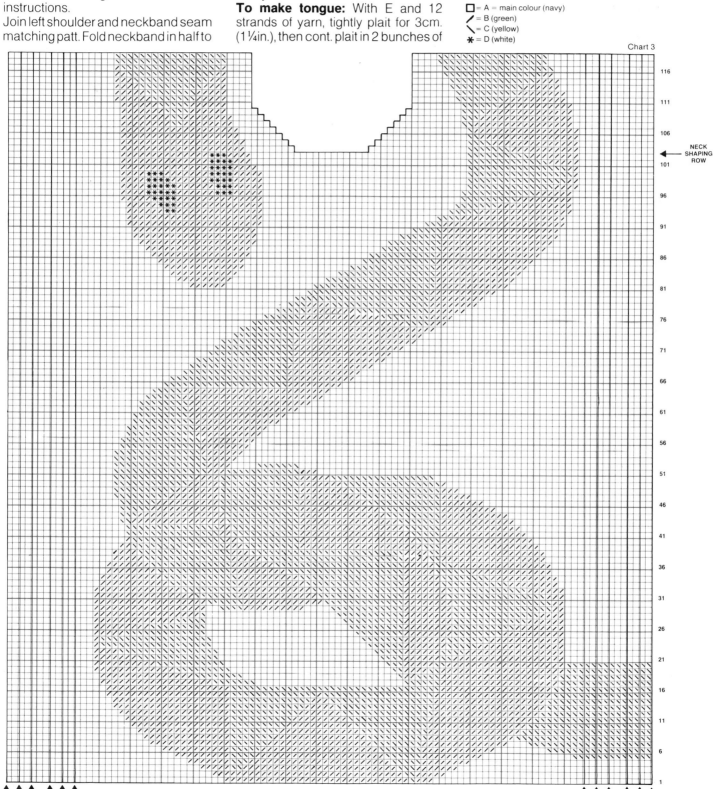

NECK
SHAPING
ROW

116
111
106
101
96
91
86
81
76
71
66
61
56
51
46
41
36
31
26
21
16
11
6
1

44 42 40   38 36 34

34 36 38   40 42 44

Counting Sheep

MATERIALS

7(7: 8) 25g balls of DOUBLE KNITTING yarn in main colour, green (A).
2 balls in 2nd colour, cream (B).
1 ball in 3rd colour; black (C).
1 pair each of 3¼mm. (No. 10) and 4mm. (No. 8) knitting needles.
12 very small beads for eyes.
2 stitch holders.
The quantities of yarn given are based on average requirements and are therefore approximate.

How many sheep are there in the picture? Whatever the answer, this woolly jumper, modelled here by Saethryd Brandreth (who's a lamb), will have people flocking round in admiration.

MEASUREMENTS

To fit chest: 56(61: 66)cm. (22(24: 26)in.)
Actual measurement: 60(66: 71)cm. (24(26: 28)in.)

Length from shoulder: 38(40: 43)cm. (15(16: 17)in.)
Sleeve length: 28(33: 38)cm. (11(13: 15)in.)
Figures in brackets refer to the larger sizes. Where only one figure is given this refers to all sizes.

TENSION

22 sts. and 28 rows to 10cm. (4in.) on 4mm. needles over st. st.

ABBREVIATIONS

K = knit; **P** = purl; **st.(s.)** = stitch(es); **st. st.** = stocking stitch; **foll.** = following; **inc.** = increase; **dec.** = decrease; **cont.** = continue; **RS** = right side; **WS** = wrong side; **rep.** = repeat; **rem.** = remaining; **A** = main colour; **B,C** = contrast colours; **mm.** = millimetres; **cm.** = centimetres; **in.** = inches.

INSTRUCTIONS

Back

With 3¼mm. needles and A, cast on 54(60:66)sts. and work in K1, P1, rib for 18 rows.
Change to 4mm. needles.
Increase row: K4(7: 10), inc. in next st., *K3, inc. in next st., rep. from * to last 5(8: 11)sts., K to end of row. (66(72: 78)sts.)
Next row: P.
Now starting with a K row work straight in st. st. for 8(10: 12) rows, thus ending with a WS row.

Place chart

1st row: K2(5: 8) A, work across the 42 sts. from 1st row of **Chart 1**, K22(25: 28)A.
The chart is now set. Cont. to follow chart until the 28 rows have been worked.
Now starting with a K row work straight in st. st. for 6(8: 10) rows, thus ending with a WS row.

Place chart

1st row: K22(25:28)A, work across the 42 sts. from 1st row of **Chart 2**, K2(5: 8)A.
The chart is now set. Cont. to follow chart until the 28 rows have been worked. **
Now starting with a K row work straight in st. st. in A until back measures 37(39: 42)cm. (14½(15½: 16½)in.) from cast-on edge, ending with a WS row.

Shape back neck

Next row: K22(25: 28)sts., turn and cont. on this first set of sts. only, placing rem. sts. on a stitch holder.
*** Dec. 1 st. at neck edge on next 3 rows.
Cast off rem. 19(22: 25) sts. fairly

loosely.
Return to rem. sts. and slip first 22 sts. onto stitch holder. With RS facing rejoin yarn to rem. sts. and K to end of row.
Now work as for first side from *** to end.

Front

Work as for back to **
Now, starting with a K row, work a few rows straight in st. st. in A until front measures 32(34: 37)cm. (12½(13½: 14½)in.) from cast-on edge, ending with a WS row.

Shape front neck

Next row: K27(30: 33)sts., turn and cont. on this first set of sts. only, placing rem. sts. on a stitch holder.
**** Dec. 1 st. at neck edge on every row until 19(22: 25)sts. remain.
Now cont. straight in st. st. until front measures the same as back to shoulder cast-off edge, ending with a WS row.
Cast off all sts. fairly loosely.
Return to rem. sts. and slip first 12 sts. onto stitch holder. With RS facing rejoin yarn to rem. sts. and K to end of row.
Now work as for first side from **** to end.

Sleeves

With 3¼mm. needles and A, cast on 36 sts. and work in K1, P1, rib for 18 rows
Change to 4mm. needles.
Increase row: *K1, inc. in next st., rep. from * to end. (54 sts.)
Now starting with a P row cont. in st. st., **at the same time**, inc. 1 st. at each end of every foll. 6th row until there are 62(66: 70)sts. on the needle, ending with a WS row.

Place chart

(N.B. – work from **Chart 1** on one sleeve and **Chart 2** on the other sleeve.)
Next row: K10(12: 14)A, work across the 42 sts. from 1st row of either **Chart 1** or **Chart 2** K10(12: 14)A.
The chart is now set. Cont. to follow chart until the 28 rows have been worked, **at the same time**, work incs. as before on every foll. 6th row until there are 66(72: 78)sts. on the needle.
Now cont. straight in st. st. in A until sleeve measures 28(33: 38)cm. (11(13: 15)in.) from cast-on edge, ending with a WS row.
Cast off all sts. fairly loosely.

Neckband

Join right shoulder seam.
With 3¼mm. needles and A and RS facing, pick up and K17 sts. down left front neck, K12 sts. from stitch holder, pick up and K17 sts. up right front neck, K4 sts. down right back neck, K22 sts. from stitch holder and finally pick up and K4 sts. up left back neck. (76 sts.)
Work in K1, P1, rib for 12 rows.
Cast off fairly loosely ribwise.

TO MAKE UP

Press according to ball band instructions.
Join left shoulder and neckband seam. Fold neckband in half to inside and slip stitch loosely in position. Measure and mark 17(18: 19)cm. (6½(7: 7½)in.) each side of shoulder seam and sew sleeves between these marks. Using a chain stitch and C embroider the legs of the sheep, then using a running stitch, embroider numbers as shown in picture. Sew on beads for eyes. Join side and sleeve seams.

/ = A = main colour (green)
□ = B (cream)
\ = C (black)

Chart 1

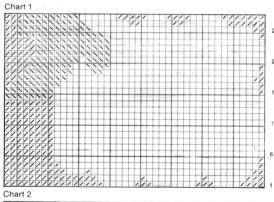

Chart 2

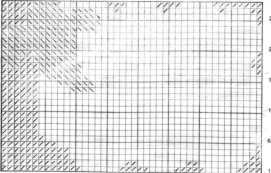

Fruit Salad

This cotton top's ideal for wearing on blazing days under a tropical sun, or, in a colder climate, with a shirt underneath. We couldn't fix a blazing day under a tropical sun for the brilliant and beautiful Sarah Kennedy; she had to make do with cool autumn weather. She brought her own shirt and her own supply of sunshine.

MATERIALS

2 50g balls in COTTON DK in each of 4 colours: white (A), yellow (C), dark green (E) and purple (G).
1 ball in each of 3 other colours: orange (B), red (D) and emerald green (F).
20 small square buttons or beads.
Small amount of black yarn.
1 pair each of 3¼mm. (No. 10) and 4mm. (No. 8) knitting needles.
2 stitch holders.
The quantities of yarn given are based on average requirements and are therefore approximate.

MEASUREMENTS

To fit bust: 86(91: 96: 101: 106)cm. (34(36: 38: 40: 42)in.)
Actual measurement: 90(96: 100: 106: 110)cm. (36(38½: 40: 42½: 44)in.)
Length from shoulder: 52cm (20½in.)
Figures in brackets refer to the larger sizes. Where only one figure is given this refers to all sizes.

TENSION

20 sts. and 26 rows to 10cm. (4in.) on 4mm. needles over st. st.

ABBREVIATIONS

K = knit; **P** = purl; **st.(s.)** = stitch(es); **st. st.** = stocking stitch; **patt.** = pattern; **cont.** = continue; **RS** = right side; **WS** = wrong side; **beg.** = beginning; **dec.** = decrease; **foll.** = following; **rem.** = remaining; **alt.** = alternate; **A,B,C, D,E,F,G** = contrast colours; **DK** = double knitting; **mm.** = millimetres; **cm.** = centimetres; **in.** = inches.

INSTRUCTIONS

Back
With 3¼mm. needles and A, cast on 90(96: 100: 106: 110)sts. and work in K1, P1, rib for 4 rows.
Change to 4mm. needles.
Now starting with the 1st row work in st. st. from chart, working between appropriate lines for size required.
Cont. straight as set until 70th row of chart has been worked, thus ending

with a WS row.

Shape armholes

Keeping chart correct, cast off 5(7: 8: 10: 11)sts. at beg. of next 2 rows. Now dec. 1 st. at each end of next 8 rows, and then at each end of next row and 3 foll. 4th rows. (56(58: 60: 62: 64)sts.) Now cont. straight following chart until 110th row of chart has been worked, thus ending with a WS row.

Shape back neck

Next row: (111th row of chart) Patt. 23(24: 25: 26: 27)sts., turn and cont. on this first set of sts. only, placing rem. sts. on a stitch holder. ** Keeping chart correct, dec. 2 sts. loosely at neck edge on next 2 rows. then dec. 1 st. at neck edge on next 5 rows. Dec. 1 st. at neck edge on next row and 3 foll. alt. rows. (10(11: 12: 13: 14)sts.) Now work 5 rows straight in st. st. (130 rows of chart complete).
Cast off all sts. fairly loosely.
Return to rem. sts. and slip first 10 sts. onto stitch holder. With RS facing rejoin yarn to rem. sts. and patt. to end of row.
Now work as for first side from ** to end.

Front

Work exactly as for back.

Neckband

Join right shoulder seam.

With 3¼mm. needles and A and RS facing, pick up and K23 sts. down left front neck, K10 sts. from stitch holder, pick up and K23 sts. up right front neck, K23 sts. down right back neck, K10 sts. from stitch holder and finally pick up and K23 sts. up left back neck. (112 sts.)
Work in K1, P1, rib for 4 rows.
Cast off fairly loosely ribwise.

Armbands (alike)

Join left shoulder and neckband seam.
With 3¼mm. needles and A and RS facing, pick up and K110(116: 120: 126: 130)sts. evenly all around armhole edge.
Work in K1, P1, rib for 4 rows.
Cast off fairly loosely ribwise.

TO MAKE UP

Press according to ball band instructions.
Sew on beads and embroider cherry, orange and grapefruit stalks with black yarn as in picture.
Carefully sew side and armband seams.

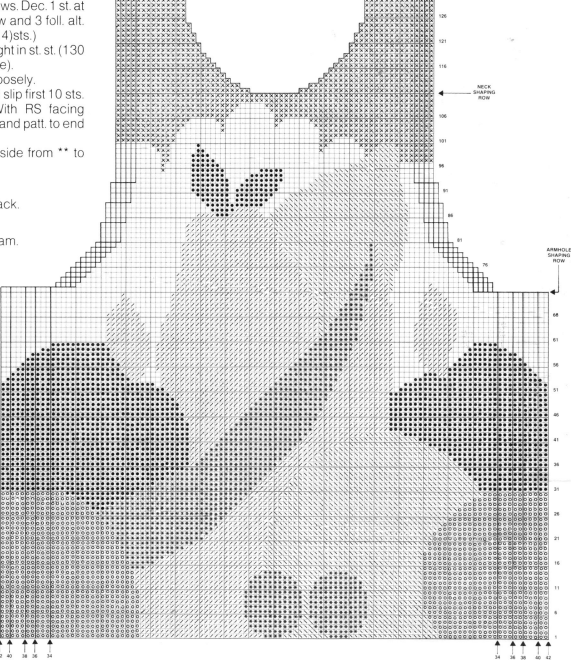

X = A (white)
o = B (orange)
\ = C (yellow)
* = D (red)
/ = E (dark green)
● = F (emerald green)
□ = G (purple)

Friendly Ghosts

I think this could be a fashion sensation from ghost to ghost! The joy of the spooks on this fun knit is that they're so friendly. The model is Aphra Brandreth who is very friendly too.

TENSION

22 sts. and 28 rows to 10cm. (4in.) on 4mm. needles over st. st.

MATERIALS

7(8: 9) 25g balls of DOUBLE KNITTING yarn in main colour charcoal grey (A).
1 ball in each of 2 other colours, white (B) and yellow (C).
Small amount of black yarn to embroider smiles.
1 pair each of 3¼mm. (No. 10) and 4mm. (No. 8) knitting needles.
4 small black beads or buttons for eyes.
2 stitch holders.
The quantities of yarn given are based on average requirements and are therefore approximate.

MEASUREMENTS

To fit chest: 56(61: 66)cm. (22(24: 26)in.)
Actual measurement: 60(66: 71)cm. (24(26: 28)in.)
Length from shoulder: 38(40: 43)cm. (15(16: 17)in.)
Sleeve length: 28(33: 38)cm. (11(13: 15)in.)
Figures in brackets refer to the larger sizes. Where only one figure is given this refers to all sizes.

ABBREVIATIONS

K = knit; **P** = purl; **st.(s.)** = stitch(es); **st. st.** = stocking stitch; **foll.** = following; **inc.** = increase; **dec.** = decrease; **cont.** = continue; **RS** = right side; **WS** = wrong side; **rep.** = repeat; **rem.** = remaining; **A** = main colour; **B,C** = contrast colours; **mm.** = millimetres; **cm.** = centimetres; **in.** = inches.
Note
The outline of the smaller ghost worked in A may be embroidered or swiss-darned when work is complete rather than knitted, if preferred.

INSTRUCTIONS

Back

With 3¼mm. needles and A, cast on 54(60:66)sts. and work in K1, P1, rib for 18 rows.
Change to 4mm. needles.
Increase row: K4(7: 10), inc. in next st., *K3, inc. in next st., rep. from * to last 5(8: 11)sts., K to end of row. (66(72: 78)sts.)
Next row: P. **
Now starting with a K row work straight in st. st. in A until back measures 37(39: 42)cm. (14½(15½: 16½)in.) from cast-on edge, ending with a WS row.

Shape back neck
Next row: K22(25: 28)sts., turn and cont. on this first set of sts. only, placing rem. sts. on a stitch holder.
*** Dec. 1 st. at neck edge on next 3 rows.
Cast off rem. 19(22: 25)sts. fairly loosely.
Return to rem. sts. and slip first 22 sts. onto stitch holder. With RS facing rejoin yarn to rem. sts. and K to end of row.
Now work as for first side from *** to end.

Front

Work as for back to **
Place chart
Start working from chart from appropriate row as indicated for size required.
Next row: (RS facing – 13th(7th: 1st) row of chart) K2(5: 8)A, work across the 62 sts. of appropriate row of chart, K2(5: 8)A. The chart is now set. Cont. to follow chart until row 82 of chart has been completed, thus ending with a WS row.
Now work straight in st. st. in A only until front measures 32(34: 37)cm. (12½(13½: 14½)in.) from cast-on edge, ending with a WS row.

Shape front neck
Next row: K27(30: 33)sts., turn and cont. on this first set of sts. only, placing rem. sts. on a stitch holder.
****Dec. 1 st. at neck edge on every row until 19(22: 25)sts. remain. Now cont. straight in st. st. until front measures the same as back to shoulder cast-off edge, ending with a WS row.
Cast off all sts. fairly loosely.
Return to rem. sts. and slip first 12 sts. onto stitch holder, with RS facing rejoin

yarn to rem. sts. and K to end of row.
Work as for first side from **** to end.

Sleeves

With 3¼mm. needles and A, cast on 36 sts. and work in K1, P1, rib for 18 rows.
Change to 4mm. needles.
Increase row: *K1, inc. in next st., rep from * to end. (54 sts.)
Now starting with a P row cont. in st. st. in A, **at the same time**, inc. 1 st. at each end of every foll. 6th row until there are 66(72: 78) sts. on the needle.
Now cont. straight in st. st. until sleeve measures 28(33: 38)cm. (11(13: 15)in.) from cast-on edge, ending with a WS row.
Cast off all sts. fairly loosely.

Neckband

Join right shoulder seam.
With 3¼mm. needles and A and RS facing, pick up and K17 sts. down left front neck, K12 sts. from stitch holder, pick up and K17 sts. up right front neck, K4 sts. down right back neck, K22 sts. from stitch holder, and finally pick up and K4 sts. up left back neck (76 sts.)
Work in K1, P1, rib for 12 rows.
Cast off fairly loosely ribwise.

TO MAKE UP

Press according to ball band instructions.
Join left shoulder and neckband seam. Fold neckband in half to inside and slip stitch loosely in position. Measure and mark 17(18: 19)cm. (6½(7: 7½)in.) each side of shoulder seam and sew sleeves between these marks. Embroider the ghosts' smiles with black yarn and sew on beads or buttons for eyes as in picture. Join side and sleeve seams.

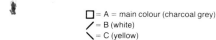

□ = A = main colour (charcoal grey)
╱ = B (white)
╲ = C (yellow)

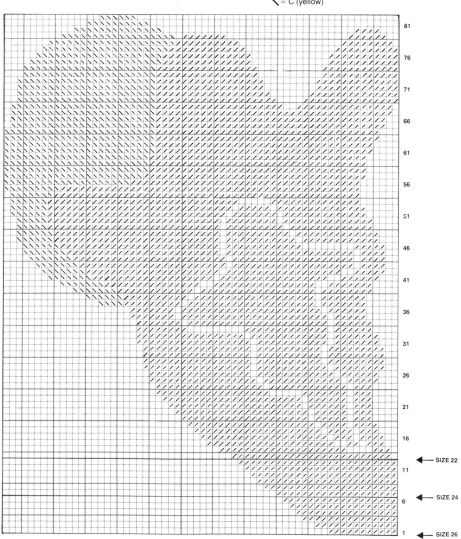

Jewel in the Jigsaw

Lynsey de Paul
Isn't that tall
But her talent's quite gigantic.
In her mohair sweater
There's nobody better
At driving the men quite frantic!

MATERIALS

4(4: 4: 5: 5: 5) 50g balls of PATONS VISION in black, 1st colour (A).
3(3: 4: 4: 4: 5) balls in yellow, contrast colour (B).
1 pair each of 4½mm. (No. 7) and 6mm. (No. 4) knitting needles.
2 stitch holders.
The quantities of yarn given are based on average requirements and are therefore approximate.

MEASUREMENTS

To fit bust/chest: 86(91: 96: 101: 107: 112)cm. (34(36: 38: 40: 42: 44)in.)
Actual measurement: 92(97: 103: 106: 112: 117)cm. (36½(39: 41: 42: 44½: 47)in.)
Length from shoulder: 64(67: 70: 72: 72: 72)cm. (25½(26½: 27½: 28½: 28½: 28½)in.)
Sleeve length: 48(48: 48: 51: 51: 51)cm. (19(19: 19: 20: 20: 20)in.)
Figures in brackets refer to the larger sizes. Where only one figure is given this refers to all sizes.

TENSION

14 sts. and 19 rows to 10cm. (4in.) on 6mm. needles over st. st.

ABBREVIATIONS

K = knit; **P** = purl; **st.(s.)** = stitch(es); **st. st.** = stocking stitch; **patt.** = pattern; **foll.** = following; **inc.** = increase; **dec.** = decrease; **cont.** = continue; **RS** = right side; **WS** = wrong side; **rep.** = repeat; **rem.** = remaining; **A,B** = contrast colours; **mm.** = millimetres; **cm.** = centimetres; **in.** = inches.

Note
When working in colour pattern use a separate ball of yarn for each colour area worked twisting yarns together on wrong side at joins to avoid making a hole.

INSTRUCTIONS

Back
With 4½mm. needles and A, cast on 56(58: 60: 62: 64: 66)sts., and work in K1, P1, rib for 16 rows.
Change to 6mm. needles.
Increase row: K10(6: 2: 14: 12: 10), inc. in next st., *K4(4: 4: 2: 2: 2), inc. in next st., rep. from * to last 10(6: 2: 14: 12: 10)sts., K to end of row (64(68: 72: 74: 78: 82)sts.)
Next row: P.
Now starting with a K row work in st. st. in the following pattern:
Foundation row: K, A17(18: 19: 19: 20: 21), B30(32: 34: 36: 38: 40), A17(18: 19: 19: 20: 21).
Starting with a P row, work 15(17: 19: 21: 21: 21) rows as set in st. st.

Now cont. in colour patt. and st. st. as follows:

1st row: A23(24: 25: 25: 26: 27), B18(20:22:24:26:28), A23(24:25:25: 26: 27:).

2nd row: A25(26: 27: 27: 28: 29), B14(16:18:20:22:24), A25(26:27:27: 28: 29).

3rd row: A26(27: 28: 28: 29: 30), B12(14:16:18:20:22), A26(27:28:28: 29: 30).

4th row: As 3rd row.

5th row: A27(28: 29: 29: 30: 31), B10(12:14:16:18:20), A27(28:29:29: 30: 31).

Work last row 5 times more, keeping st. st. correct.

11th and 12th rows: As 3rd row.

13th row: As 2nd row.

14th row: As 1st row.

Work 6 foundation rows, keeping st. st. correct.

21st row: B2, A15(16: 17: 17: 18: 19), B30(32: 34: 36: 38: 40), A15(16:17:17: 18: 19), B2.

22nd row: B3, A14(15: 16: 16: 17: 18), B30(32:34:36:38:40), A14(15:16:16: 17: 18), B3.

23rd row: B4, A13(14: 15: 15: 16: 17), B30(32:34:36:38:40), A13(14:15:15: 16: 17), B4.

Work last row 3 times more.

27th row: B5, A12(13: 14: 14: 15: 16), B30(32:34:36:38:40), A12(13:14:14: 15: 16), B5.

Work last row 7 times more.

35th row: B17(18: 19: 19: 20: 21), A10(11: 12: 13: 14: 15), B10, A10(11: 12:13:14:15), B17(18:19:19:20:21).

Work last row 7 times more.

43rd row: B17(18: 19: 19: 20: 21), A11(12:13:14:15:16), B8, A11(12:13: 14: 15: 16), B17(18: 19: 19: 20: 21).

Work last row 3 times more.

47th row: B17(18: 19: 19: 20: 21), A12(13:14:15:16:17), B6, A12(13:14: 15: 16: 17), B17(18: 19: 19: 20: 21).

48th row: B17(18: 19: 19: 20: 21), A13(14:15:16:17:18), B4, A13(14:15: 16: 17: 18), B17(18: 19: 19: 20: 21).

49th row: B17(18: 19: 19: 20: 21), A30(32:34:36:38:40), B17(18:19:19: 20: 21).

Work last row 5 times more.

55th row: B11(12: 13: 13: 14: 15), A42(44:46:48:50:52), B11(12:13:13: 14: 15).

56th row: B9(10: 11: 11: 12: 13), A46(48: 50: 52: 54: 56), B9(10: 11: 11: 12: 13).

57th row: B8(9:10:10:11:12), A48(50: 52: 54: 56: 58), B8(9: 10: 10: 11: 12).

58th row: As 57th row.

59th row: B7(8: 9: 9: 10: 11), A50(52: 54: 56: 58: 60), B7(8: 9: 9: 10: 11).

Work last row 5 times more.

65th and 66th rows: As 57th row.

67th row: As 56th row.

68th row: As 55th row.

69th and 70th rows: As 49th row.

Now rep. the 49th row and work straight until back measures 62(65: 68: 70: 70: 70)cm. (24½(25½: 26½: 27½:27½:27½)in.) from cast-on edge, ending with a WS row.

Shape back neck

Next row: K23(25: 27: 28: 30: 32)sts., turn and cont. on this first set of sts. only, placing rem. sts. on a stitch holder.

** Keeping patt. correct, dec. 1 st. at neck edge on next 3 rows.

Cast off rem. 20(22: 24: 25: 27: 29)sts. fairly loosely.

Return to rem. sts. and slip first 18 sts. onto stitch holder. With RS facing rejoin yarn to rem. sts. and patt. to end of row.

Now work as for first side from ** to end.

Front

Work as for back until front measures 56(59: 62: 64: 64: 64)cm. (22(23: 24: 25: 25: 25)in.) from cast-on edge, ending with a WS row.

Shape front neck

Next row: K26(28: 30: 31: 33: 35)sts., turn and cont. on this first set of sts. only, placing rem. sts. on a stitch holder.

*** Keeping patt. correct, dec. 1 st. at neck edge on every row until 20(22: 24: 25: 27: 29)sts. remain.

Now cont. straight in patt. until front measures the same as back to cast-off shoulder edge, ending with a WS row.

Cast off all sts. fairly loosely.

Return to rem. sts. and slip first 12 sts. onto stitch holder. With RS facing rejoin yarn to rem. sts. and patt. to end of row.

Now work as for first side from *** to end.

Sleeves

With 4½mm. needles and B, cast on 28 sts. and work in K1, P1, rib for 16 rows. Change to 6mm. needles.

Increase row: *K1, inc. in next st., rep. from * to end. (42 sts.)

Starting with a P row work 3 rows in st. st.

Now cont. in colour patt. and st. st. as follows:

1st row: Inc. in 1st st., B18, A4, B18, inc. in last st.

2nd row: B19, A6, B19.

3rd row: B18, A8, B18.

4th row: As 3rd row.

5th row: Inc. in 1st st., B17, A8, B17, inc. in last st.

6th row: B19, A8, B19.

7th row: B18, A10, B18.

8th row: As 7th row.

9th row: Inc. in 1st st. B17: A10, B17, inc. in last st.

10th row: B19, A10, B19.

11th and 12th rows: As 10th row.

Now cont. in A in st. st., inc. 1 st. at each end of 3rd row and every foll. 4th row as set until there are 68sts. on the needle, ending with a WS row.

51st row: B14, A10, B20, A10, B14.

52nd row: As 51st row.

53rd row: Inc. in 1st st., B13, A10, B20, A10, B13, inc. in last st.

54th row: B15, A10, B20, A10, B15.

Work last row 4 times more.

59th row: B16, A8, B22, A8, B16.

Work last row 3 times more.

63rd row: B17, A6, B24, A6, B17.

64th row: B18, A4, B26, A4, B18.

Now cont. straight in B only until sleeve measures 48(48: 48: 51: 51: 51)cm. (19(19: 19: 20: 20: 20)in.) from cast-on edge, ending with a WS row.

Cast off all sts. fairly loosely.

Neckband

Join right shoulder seam.

With 4½mm. needles and A and RS facing, pick up and K14 sts. down left front neck, K12 sts. from stitch holder, pick up and K14 sts. up right front neck, K4 sts. down right back neck, K18 sts. from stitch holder and finally pick up and K4 sts. up left back neck. (66 sts.)

Work in K1, P1, rib for 10 rows.

Cast off fairly loosely ribwise.

TO MAKE UP

Press according to ball band instructions. Join left shoulder and neckband seam. Fold neckband in half to inside and slip stitch loosely in position. Measure and mark 27cm. (10½in.) each side of shoulder seam and sew sleeves between these marks. Join side and sleeve seams, matching pattern.

Pig Family

very member of the family can have – should have – a
pig jumper. They are easy to knit and great fun to
wear – with real tails you can actually tweak! As you can
see the *Knitability* pig family is being modelled by the
Brandreth family … apart from one little piggy who got
away.

MATERIALS

3(3: 3: 4: 4: 4: 5: 5: 5: 6: 7: 7) 25g balls of DOUBLE KNITTING yarn in 1st colour (A).
5(6: 6: 7: 8: 10: 10: 10: 11: 11: 12: 12) balls in 2nd colour (B).
1(1: 1: 1: 1: 1: 1: 1: 1: 2: 2: 2) ball(s) in 3rd colour (C).
1 ball in 4th colour (D).
1 pair each of 3¼mm. (No. 10) and 4mm. (No. 8) knitting needles.
1 medium size crochet hook.
2 stitch holders.
The quantities of yarn given are based on average requirements and are therefore approximate.

MEASUREMENTS

To fit chest/bust: 56(61: 66: 71: 76: 81: 86: 91: 96: 101: 107: 112)cm. (22(24: 26: 28: 30: 32: 34: 36: 38: 40: 42: 44)in.)
Actual measurement: 60(66: 71: 75: 80: 86: 91: 97: 102: 106: 111: 117)cm. (24(26: 28: 30: 32: 34: 36: 38: 40: 42: 44: 46)in.)
Length from shoulder: 39(41: 44: 49: 54: 59; 64: 67: 69: 72: 72: 72)cm. (15(16: 17: 19: 21: 23: 25: 26: 27: 28: 28: 28)in.)
Sleeve length: 28(33: 38: 42: 44: 47: 48: 48: 48: 51: 51: 51)cm. (11(13: 15: 16½: 17½: 18½: 19: 19: 19: 20: 20: 20)in.)
Figures in brackets refer to the larger sizes. Where only one figure is given this refers to all sizes.

TENSION

22 sts. and 28 rows to 10cm. (4in.) on 4mm. needles over st. st.

ABBREVIATIONS

K = knit; **P** = purl; **st.(s.)** = stitch(es); **st. st.** = stocking stitch; **foll.** = following; **inc.** = increase; **dec.** = decrease; **cont.** = continue; **RS** = right side; **WS** = wrong side; **rep.** = repeat; **rem.** = remaining; **A,B,C,D** = contrast colours; **mm.** = millimetres; **cm.** = centimetres; **in.** = inches.

INSTRUCTIONS

Back

With 3¼mm. needles and A, cast on 54(60: 66: 70: 76: 82: 82: 88: 94: 98: 104: 110)sts. and work in K1, P1, rib for 14(14: 14: 16: 16: 16: 18: 18: 18: 18: 18: 18) rows.

Change to 4mm. needles.
Increase row: K4(7: 10: 12: 15: 18: 6: 9: 12: 14: 17: 20), inc. in next st., *K3, inc. in next st., rep. from * to last 5(8: 11: 13: 16: 19: 7: 10: 13: 15: 18: 21)sts., K to end of row.
(66(72: 78: 82: 88: 94: 100: 106: 112: 116: 122: 128)sts.)
Next row: P.
Now starting with a K row work 16(16: 16: 26: 26: 26: 36: 36: 36: 46: 46: 46) rows straight in st. st. in A.
Break off A and cont. in B as follows:
Place chart
Next row: (RS facing) With B, K18(21: 24: 24: 27: 30: 30: 33: 36: 36: 39: 42)sts., work across the 30(30: 30: 34: 34: 34: 40: 40: 40: 44: 44: 44)sts. from 1st row of appropriate chart for size required, then with B K rem. 18(21: 24: 24: 27: 30: 30: 33: 36: 36: 39: 42)sts.
The chart is now set. Cont. to work the 42(42: 42: 48: 48: 48: 56: 56: 56: 62: 62: 62) rows of chart, but **DO NOT** work the face features. ******
When the chart is complete cont. straight in st. st. in B until back measures 37(39: 42: 47: 52: 57: 62: 65: 67: 70: 70: 70)cm. (14½(15½: 16½: 18½: 20½: 22½: 24½: 25½: 26½: 27½: 27½: 27½)in.) from cast-on edge, ending with a WS row.
Shape back neck
Next row: K22(25: 28: 28: 31: 34: 35: 38: 41: 43: 46: 49)sts., turn and cont. on this first set of sts. only, placing rem. sts. on a stitch holder.
*** Dec. 1 st. at neck edge on next 3 rows.
Cast off rem. 19(22: 25: 25: 28: 31: 32: 35: 38: 40: 43: 46) sts. fairly loosely.
Return to rem. sts. and slip first 22(22: 22: 26: 26: 26: 30: 30: 30: 30: 30: 30)sts. onto stitch holder. With RS facing rejoin yarn to rem. sts. and K to end of row.
Now work as for first side from ******* to end.

Front

Work as for back to ******, but **WORK ALL** face features as shown on chart.
When chart is complete cont. straight in st. st. in B until front measures 32(34: 37: 42: 47: 52: 56: 59: 61: 64: 64: 64)cm. (12½(13½: 14½: 16½: 18½: 20½: 22: 23: 24: 25; 25: 25)in.) from cast-on edge, ending with a WS row.
Shape front neck
Next row: K27(30: 33: 34: 37: 40: 42: 45: 48: 50: 53: 56)sts., turn and cont. on this first set of sts. only, placing rem. sts. on a stitch holder.
**** Dec. 1 st. at neck edge on every row until 19(22: 25: 25: 28: 31: 32: 35: 38: 40: 43: 46)sts. remain.
Now cont. straight until front measures the same as back to shoulder cast-off edge, ending with a WS row.
Cast off all sts. fairly loosely.
Return to rem. sts. and slip first 12(12: 12: 14: 14: 14: 16: 16: 16: 16: 16: 16)sts. onto stitch holder. With RS facing rejoin yarn to rem. sts. and K to end of row.
Now work as for first side from ******** to end.

Sleeves

With 3¼mm. needles and A, cast on 36(36: 36: 40: 40: 40: 44: 44: 44: 44: 44: 44)sts., and work in K1, P1, rib for 14(14: 14: 16: 16: 18: 18: 18: 18: 18: 18) rows.
Change to 4mm. needles.
Increase row: K1(1: 1: 2: 2: 2: 2: 2: 2: 2: 2: 2), inc. in next st., *K1, inc. in next st., rep. from * to last 0(0: 0: 3: 3: 3: 3: 3: 3: 3: 3: 3)sts., K to end. (54(54: 54: 58: 58: 58: 64: 64: 64: 64: 64: 64)sts.)
Now starting with a P row work in st. st. in A, **at the same time**, inc. 1 st. at each end of every foll. 6th row until there are 62(62: 62: 68: 68: 68: 74: 74: 74: 74: 74: 74)sts. on the needle, ending with a WS row.
Change to B and cont. to inc. as before on every foll. 6th row until there are 66(72: 78: 80: 84: 88: 94: 94: 94: 100: 100: 100)sts. on the needle.
Now work straight in st. st. in B until sleeve measures 28(33: 38: 42: 44: 47: 48: 48: 48: 51: 51: 51)cm. (11(13: 15: 16½: 17½: 18½: 19: 19: 19: 20: 20: 20)in.) from cast-on edge, ending with a WS row.
Cast off all sts. fairly loosely.

Neckband

Join right shoulder seam.
With 3¼mm. needles and A and RS facing, pick up and K17(17: 17: 18: 18: 18: 21: 21: 21: 21: 21: 21)sts. down left front neck, K12(12: 12: 14: 14: 14: 16: 16: 16: 16: 16: 16)sts. from stitch holder, pick up and K17(17: 17: 18: 18: 18: 21: 21: 21: 21: 21: 21)sts. up right front neck, K4 sts. down right back neck, K22(22: 22: 26: 26: 26: 30: 30: 30: 30: 30: 30)sts. from stitch holder and finally pick up and K4 sts. up left back neck. (76(76: 76: 84: 84: 84: 96: 96: 96: 96: 96: 96)sts.)

Work in K1, P1, rib for 12 rows.
Cast off fairly loosely ribwise.

TO MAKE UP

Press according to ball band instructions.
Join left shoulder and neckband seam. Fold neckband in half to inside and slip stitch loosely in position. Measure and mark 17(18:19:19:20:21:23:23:23:24:24:24)cm. 6½(7:7½:7½:8:8½:9:9:9:9½:9½:9½)in. each side of shoulder seam and sew sleeves between these marks. Join side and sleeve seams. **Piggy tail:** With the medium size crochet hook and C, make 20 chains, then work single crochet st. into every loop, starting at the loop nearest the needle. The tail will curl up as you work. Tie ends together and sew in place on back.

Chart 1

Chart 2

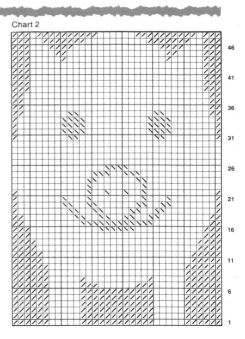

A is used for the lower part of the sweaters and cuffs and does not appear on the chart.
/ = B (main colour)
□ = C (pig colour)
\ = D (face features colour)

Chart 3

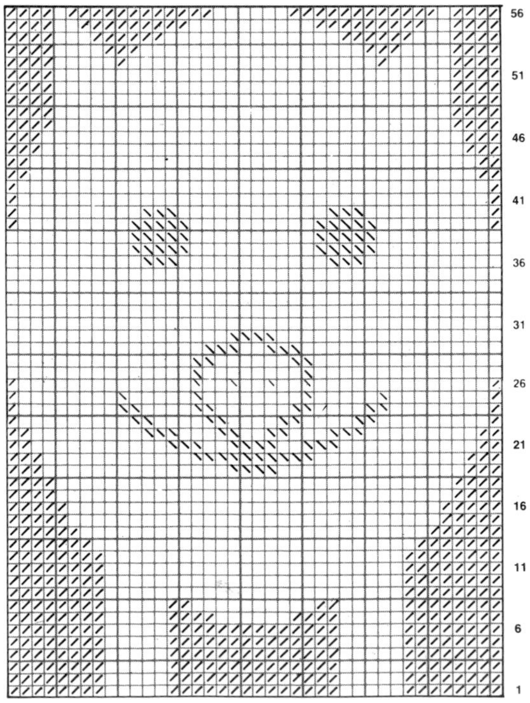

Chart 4

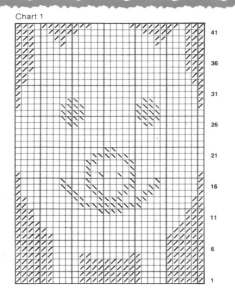

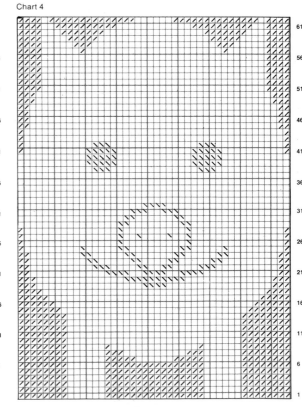